ANTISEMITISM, MISOGYNY, &
THE LOGIC OF CULTURAL
DIFFERENCE

ANTISEMITISM, MISOGYNY, & THE LOGIC OF CULTURAL DIFFERENCE
•
CESARE LOMBROSO & MATILDE SERAO

by

Nancy A. Harrowitz

University of Nebraska Press

Lincoln & London

The paper in this book meets the minimum
requirements of American National Standard for
Information Sciences — Permanence of Paper
for Printed Library Materials,
ANSI Z39.48-1984

Library of Congress
Cataloging in Publication Data
Harrowitz, Nancy, 1952-
Antisemitism, misogyny, and the logic
of cultural difference: Cesare Lombroso and
Matilde Serao / Nancy A. Harrowitz.
p. cm. – (Texts and contexts; v.10)
Includes bibliographical references and
index. ISBN0-8032-2374-9
1. Serao, Matilde, 1856-1927 – Criticism
and interpretation.
2. Lombroso, Cesare, 1835-1909 –
Influence.
3. Antisemitism in literature.
4. Misogyny in literature.
I . Title. II. Series.
PQ4841.E7Z84   1994
853'.8–dc20
93-44322
CIP

In loving memory of my brother

Michael Edward Harrowitz

CONTENTS

ACKNOWLEDGMENTS

I wish to thank the Boston University Humanities Foundation for the Junior Fellowship I was awarded in 1990–1991, which greatly aided in the writing of this book. I would also like to thank *Stanford Italian Review* for permission to reprint sections of my article, 'Matilde Serao's *La mano tagliata:* Figuring the Material in Mystery,' *Stanford Italian Review* 7, 1988.

All translations, unless otherwise indicated, are mine. My warmest appreciation to my colleagues and friends who so generously gave their time and criticism in reading early drafts of chapters: Barbara Spackman, Katherine O'Connor, T. Jefferson Kline, and Fiora Bassanese; and to the others with whom I had helpful conversations about the project in particular and writing in general: Keala Jewell, Melissa Zeiger, and Kathe Darr. I especially wish to acknowledge my debt to Sander Gilman, whose intellectual leadership in the field of cultural studies has been inspirational. My husband, Craig Haller, for his infinite patience during the writing of this book and his technical help in producing the manuscript, deserves more than thanks.

CHAPTER ONE

THE TAINT OF THE QUAGGA: A RELATION OF RACE, SCIENCE, & LITERATURE

O nce upon a time there was an animal known as the quagga. Similar in its striping to a zebra, the quagga became extinct in the last part of the nineteenth century when, like the dodo, it became an object of European colonial curiosity. Before passing into extinction, however, it had attained a glory all its own through the efforts of a certain Lord Morton. And this is where our tale of a relation between race, science, and literature begins.

Morton wanted to breed some of the nearly extinct quaggas but could only obtain a male. He mated the male quagga with a nearly purebred Arabian mare, a breeding that was her first. The mare gave birth to a hybrid that looked like both parents. At this point there is nothing strange about this episode of animal husbandry. What is strange, however, is the future of this particular mare and her progeny. Morton gave the mare to an acquaintance of his, Sir Gore Ouseley, who then bred her to an Arabian stallion. Her new foals continued to resemble the quagga. Morton wrote a letter in 1820 to the Royal Society detailing the results of these experiments, which became so well known that portraits of these foals that looked like the quagga were hung in the Royal College of Surgeons in London for all the world to admire.

Such illustrious scientists as Charles Darwin, Louis Agassiz,

Claude Bernard, George John Romanes, and Herbert Spencer all subscribed to the theory of heredity 'proven' by Morton's experiments. The story of the quagga provides us with a way to illustrate some of the questions, both cultural and scientific, that were being asked at the time and to examine as well the answers that were proposed. The notion of the potential influence of the first breeding on subsequent breedings was indeed alluring, as it provided a way to privilege the role of the male and to furnish a male prerogative of influencing other progeny not actually his own.

Morton's experiment was faithfully recorded by Darwin in *The Variation of Animals and Plants Under Domestication* (1868). As Darwin tells us in the section entitled 'On the Direct Action of the Male Element on the Mother Form':

> In the case often quoted from Lord Morton, a nearly purely-bred Arabian chestnut mare bore a hybrid to a quagga; she was subsequently sent to Sir Gore Ouseley, and produced two colts by a black Arabian horse. These colts were partially dun-colored, and were striped on the legs more plainly than the real hybrid, or even than the quagga. One of the two colts had its neck and some other parts of its body plainly marked with stripes. Stripes on the body, not to mention those on the legs, are extremely rare – I speak after having long attended to the subject – with horses of all kinds in Europe, and are almost unknown in the case of Arabians. But what makes the case still more striking is that in these colts the hair of the mane resembled that of the quagga, being short, still and upright. Hence there can be no doubt that the quagga affected the character of the offspring subsequently begot by the black Arabian horse.[1]

Darwin's version of the quagga experiment is found in his theoretical and anecdotal narrative regarding the influence of what he calls the 'male element' on the female of the species. Two kinds of examples are brought together in his discussion: plants whose nonreproductive parts are exposed to foreign pollen and seem to have a reaction to it and 'animals on the subsequent progeny of the female by a second male.'[2] After giving examples from the plant world, Darwin makes the jump to the animal kingdom using the story of the quagga. The tone of Darwin's version is not ambivalent: 'hence there can be no doubt,' he says, utterly convinced of the veracity of the hypothesis.

A brief digression into animal husbandry is pertinent here. Horses beget much like human beings: there is sperm from one father that produces offspring at one time only. There is no storage of sperm or any other way whatsoever in which the father of one offspring can influence future parturitions. Two questions thus arise from this reading of the episode of Morton and his quagga and Darwin's representation of the story: Why was the experiment, as Darwin says, 'often-quoted,' as it could not have been actually true, and why does Darwin, the great biologist and theorist of evolution, fall for it hoof, line, and sinker?

In order to answer these and other questions that the story of the quagga raises, a further look at the history of the reception of the quagga breeding is in order. The theory of the purported influence of the first mating came to be called *telegony*, or 'procreation at a distance,' late in the century by the German biologist Augustus Weismann. In Richard W. Burkhardt's 'Closing the Door on Lord Morton's Mare: The Rise and Fall of Telegony,' we learn the following:

> The subject of this essay is an exceptional, alleged phenomenon that enjoyed a remarkable career in the nineteenth century. Its history is nearly the reverse of the familiar relation between anomaly and theory. Though identified as 'singular' and 'extraordinary' when it was first brought to the attention of the Royal Society in 1820, it was nonetheless widely accepted for the next seventy years. Scientists who made any pretense of understanding reproduction and heredity managed to find ways of explaining it. . . . From the vantage point of the present, the phenomenon in question qualifies as a three-time loser. Modern biology has no place for it. Histo-

ries of science fail to indicate the role it played in pre-1900 discussions of heredity. As a final insult, the classic case of the phenomenon involves a species of animal that is now extinct.[3]

Burkhardt raises several important points here: first, the singularity of the experiment in question; second, its seemingly unexplainable lure for the best scientists of the time; and third, the way in which even a widely accepted theory can rather suddenly go out of style and, like the quagga, become extinct. Who today could recognize a quagga? And who today would embrace the theory that it came to embody? The question of who today could recognize a quagga may in fact soon be anything but rhetorical: scientists are now experimenting with quagga DNA.[4]

The theory that the quagga came to represent is simple, yet its implications are deadly: the progeny of a female is forever influenced by her first breeding. Returning to Darwin, the first great publicist of the theory, we see the beginning of a pattern of acceptance that will repeat itself during the century. Darwin's notion of variability and the advantages he saw therein would provide part of an answer as to why he found the case of the quagga compelling.[5] Variability was considered a strength, an adroitness to adapt to new situations, the capability to be multifaceted. Later, however, Darwin-influenced racial scientists used variability as a weapon against women, Jews, and blacks, who were considered to be not variable 'enough.'[6]

It is difficult to look at Darwin's thought independent of his tremendous influence, an enterprise fraught with complexities and difficulties. Gillian Beer discusses the intense manipulation of Darwinian terms that occurred during the hundred years after his works appeared, and new studies, such as Carl Degler's *In Search of Human Nature: The Decline and Revival of Darwinism in American Social Thought,* examine the continuing influence of Darwin's ideas. What I will call the 'metaphorization of variability,' not surprising given the appropriation of Darwinian terms, has its corollary in another, more familial relationship: that between Darwin and his younger first cousin, Francis Galton. The seriousness of the influence of Galton's eugenics is succinctly stated by Beer, as she discusses the effect of Darwin's theories:

> During the past hundred years or so evolutionary theory has functioned in our culture like a myth in a period of belief, moving endlessly to and fro between metaphor and paradigm, feeding an extraordinary range of disciplines beyond its own original biological field. In the later nineteenth century it gave ordering assumptions to the developing subjects of anthropology, sociology and psychology and elements in its ideas have been appropriated to serve as confirming metaphors for beliefs politically at odds with those of Darwin himself, such as social Darwinism, and even – through a displaced eugenic movement – a nightmare acting out of 'artificial selection' in Nazism.[7]

Galton occupies a fascinating spot in the nineteenth-century marketplace of ideas. He is at once the inventor of a system of fingerprinting, crucial to the developing science of criminology and criminal detection, and the first theorist of eugenics. He is inextricably linked to racialist theories, both through the influence of eugenics and through his own conservative political beliefs.[8] Galton's political motivations behind the theories of eugenics are clear; unlike Darwin, who was liberal for his time, the aristocratic Galton preferred to avoid the mingling of blood of the lower classes with that of the upper.[9] Galton's ideas are emblematic of anxieties regarding the continuing influence of the quagga: Would the Arabians remain purebread with the racial taint of the quagga let loose among them? Could the female of the species, especially the human species, resist the influence of the first breeding, and who would control that very crucial mating? In a letter to Darwin dated March 31, 1870, Galton wrote, 'I congratulate you about the Quagga taint.'[10] The precise context of this remark is not known, as Darwin's corresponding letter to

Galton has been lost, but the expression 'the Quagga taint' is noteworthy: for Galton, it comes to represent the genealogical catastrophe of out-of-control breeding that lay in wait for the human race. Interestingly, the relationship of Galton to Darwin is like that of the quagga to the Arabian mare: a haunting specter of the inevitable mutability and evolution of theory itself, of the manipulation of ideas in different hands, of a rather sad and highly problematic outcome that itself went through a series of complex narrative maneuvers.

The influence of the quagga phenomenon was not limited to scientific circles. As Alberto Cavaglion points out in his article on the relationship of Italo Svevo to Otto Weininger, by the end of the century the story of the quagga had become almost a theme in Italian literature.[11] He cites two instances of its appearance: one in Svevo's novel *La coscienza di Zeno,* the other in a short story by Luigi Capuana published in 1903. As we will see, literary renditions of the story of the quagga themselves metamorphose in the process of serving the text in which they are imbedded. What happens to the quagga theory further exemplifies its significance for nineteenth-century culture.

Gabriele D'Annunzio also refers to the quagga theory in his 1892 novel, *L'innocente.* The male protagonist of the novel, Tullio Hermes, has discovered that his wife has been unfaithful and is pregnant by a well-known writer, who is Tullio's rival not only for the love of Giuliana but intellectually as well. Tullio develops a profound hatred for the fetus, calling it in his mind *intruso* ('the intruder'). Father of two daughters, Tullio fears that this child will turn out to be a boy, thus becoming *l'erede* ('the heir'). But heir to what? Could this possibly male fetus really be an heir if he is in fact biologically another man's child? Tullio tortures himself throughout the pregnancy as he mulls over this question. Using the theory if not the name of the quagga, Tullio tries to reassure himself that he would have had, at any rate, some influence on the fetus:

'Who knows if the son of Filippo Arborio won't be, as they say, *a spitting image* of myself. The arrangements would be much easier.' And I thought again about the sad desire to laugh that came to me the time I heard it said about a child (whom I definitely knew to be the product of adultery) in the presence of the legally married couple: – Looks just like his father! – And the resemblance was extraordinary, because of that mysterious law that the physiologists call the *heredity of influence*. According to that law, the child sometimes does not resemble either the father or the mother, but resembles the man who had contact prior to that of fertilization. A woman married for the second time, three years after the death of her first husband, produces children that have all the characteristics of the dead husband and do not resemble at all the man who procreated them.[12]

The case of the quagga has at this point been changed to a theoretical formula: a man who has had sexual relations with the mother at some point before procreation can affect the future children. We can hear the quagga swishing his tale of the 'heredity of influence' in the background of the D'Annunzian re-presentation.

Tullio's rationalization of the 'heredity of influence' ultimately fails, however, as he decides to murder the child, the biological sign of difference in their midst, the false heir – and it would seem to be the tension between 'heir' and 'heredity' that provokes the homicide. The child has to go because he has gray eyes, unlike Tullio or Giuliana – and eye color does not lie about heredity. Francis Galton treats the issue of the heredity of this trait in his book *Natural Inheritance* by listing it as a characteristic that, unlike many other physical characteristics such as skin color, will not blend or mix in any way.[13] This heir is thus proven to be biologically false and, according to Tullio's reasoning, has to be eliminated.

The murder is passively enacted: Tullio exposes the baby to intense cold in the hopes that he will sicken and die. His 'competition,' as he views the child, is made vulnerable and his

7

weakness as a newborn revealed through this event. What Tullio finds contemptible about the child is not only his 'otherness,' the seed of the intruder father that has produced this (to Tullio) monstrous birth, but also the fact that he can be passively killed in this manner: that he is an infant, strange, inarticulate, and different.

What is curious about this characterization of the child is that it reiterates the portrayal of the mother. Told from Tullio's perspective, the novel explores themes of female sickness and Tullio's male response to the crisis that this sickness provokes. Barbara Spackman has demonstrated that the scene of Giuliana's operation is eroticized for Tullio, as is her giving birth, which Tullio associates with an experience of amputation.[14] Tullio fears the unknown and little-understood female sexuality, a sexuality that can result in strange and horrific illness. Spackman's analysis can be extended to include the terror that this same sexuality could produce a monstrous infant. The correlation 'female sexuality/illness/monstrous birth' in this text would seem to be, according to its own strange logic, consistent. The ultimate response of Tullio to these issues is absolute rejection acted out in murder.

D'Annunzio's novel, by incorporating the shadow of the quagga into Tullio's reaction regarding the estranged infant, deepens the significance of the homicidal act of rejection and casts light on the importance of the story of the quagga as well. The quagga here stands for not only the unknown of female sexuality, that a myth of the influence of the first male on all subsequent offspring would find its literary expression in Tullio's anxiety over his wife's infidelity. The quagga represents as well the absolute rejectability of – and desire to murder – that which is strange, unknown, and ultimately terrifying about unbridled breeding and heredity. This blueprint for many of the scientific concerns of the last half of the nineteenth century explains as well the fascination of many scientists of that period with the case of the quagga.

In yet another example, Otto Weininger, in *Sex and Charac-*

ter, also raises the quagga experiment and makes the fateful leap from animal husbandry to human relations. Weininger's text was read and admired by James Joyce, who introduced it to his friend Italo Svevo, who includes a reference to Weininger in *La coscienza di Zeno* [The Confessions of Zeno]. Cavaglion, in his essay 'Svevo and Weininger (Lord Morton's Horse),' traces the genealogy of the reference, maintaining that it is an ironic view of the quagga. Insisting that Svevo's source for the story was not Darwin, whom Svevo actually cites in the text, but rather Weininger, Cavaglion establishes the twisted and ideologically charged itinerary of the tale: Svevo cites Darwin but in fact means Weininger. This movement mimics the crisis of paternity that the quagga embodies; now it is the paternity of the notion of the quagga, the paternity of paternity itself, that is muddled. This incident evinces yet another use of Darwin-as-emblem: Svevo's use of Darwin's name is automatic proof of the scientific validity of the story of the quagga. The way in which Weininger's name appears in Svevo's novel, in a later episode, is notably different.

Weininger, like others, furthers the theory that a woman's first 'mating' will influence other matings, that she is permanently marked by this event. He claims as well, on the basis of the evidence of telegony, that paternity is a problematic event: 'Paternity is a miserable deception; for it always must be shared with an infinite number of things and men. . . . White women who have had a child with a negro later often bear children to a white man, yet the children manifest unmistakable characteristics of the negro race. Flowers which have been pollinated with one type of pollen often, after many subsequent pollinations of different types, bear fruit that resembles the species with whose pollen they were once commissioned.'[15]

Weininger's debt to Darwin is clear in his juxtaposition of examples of both plants and animals. We can see in these examples the displacement of the psychological and social (the 'influence' of the 'first' male) onto an imaginary physiological event. This indeed is a corollary for much of nineteenth-century 'scientific' racism, which attempted to set up categories of the physical characteristics of race, only to fall back on metaphor.

It is the male quagga who 'taints,' to adopt Galton's vocabulary. But it is the female who bears the burden of the taint, as all future offspring are affected by the potential folly of the first mating and, according to the logic of this theory, serve as contaminated conduits to future generations. The worry about the genetic pool was, in pre-Mendelian terms, expressed through this horse tale; as Burkhardt tells us, 'The idea was consistent with Victorian social concerns about racial purity.'[16] The same kinds of worries motivated the racialist thinking so prevalent after Arthur de Gobineau's 1853 categorization of Aryan superiority in his *Essai sur l'inégalité des races humaines.* In fact, Julius Streicher, the Nazi publisher of *Der Sturmer,* a virulently antisemitic newspaper, made the following statement:[17] 'For those in the know, these are established facts: 1, The seed of a man of another race is a 'foreign protein.' During copulation, the seed is, in part or in whole, absorbed by the woman's fertile body [literally Mutterboden, mother-soil] and thus passes into the blood. A single act of intercourse between a Jew and an Aryan woman is sufficient to pollute her forever. She can never again give birth to pure-blooded Aryan children, even if she marries an Aryan.'[18] Streicher's theory seems obviously influenced or even directly generated by telegony, although the precise genealogy of his version is not known.

The position of women was clearly affected by the theory of telegony. Taken to its logical conclusions, especially by the eugenicists, the theory would have meant even stricter sexual controls for women to ensure that the crucial 'first breeding' was a proper one, one that would enhance the future development of the human race.

The portrait of women, figured as physically and sexually territorialized by the first male, was thus inextricably intertwined with the fate of the quagga. There is, I believe, a corollary to be made as well between such heredity paranoia and the figure of the Jew in racialist discourse. The paradigm of the quagga builds on the racialist discourse regarding miscegenation. The purported ability of the male Jew to 'contaminate' in terms of heredity has been well documented in the history of racialist texts. To give but one example among many, Sander Gilman cites a letter written by Karl Marx to Friedrich Engels describing the Jewish socialist Ferdinand Lassalle: 'And also the uncultivated eating and the horny lust of this 'idealist.' It is now completely clear to me that, as his skull shape and hair prove, he is a descendant of those Blacks who accompanied Moses on the exodus from Egypt.'[19] Gilman writes, 'Marx ascribes to the outsider Lassalle all of the traditional qualities associated with the Jew: a false language and rhetoric, bad manners, sexual aggressiveness, pushiness.'[20] The association of Lassalle with blacks is part of the mid-nineteenth-century preoccupation with the mulatto, Gilman informs us. Furthermore, the racial linking of Jews and blacks, claimed by Houston Stewart Chamberlain at the end of the century in *Foundations of the Nineteenth Century* (1903) but suggested long before then, makes up part of the racialist tension informing the idea of Jews 'polluting' the 'master race' that would later be appropriated by the Third Reich.

This snapshot of the Jewish Marx describing another Jew in this way belongs in the portrait gallery Gilman has given us of self-hating Jews. The quagga has brought us full circle: from a heredity paranoia to that which may most fully betray and contaminate, the rejection of self. Juan Comas has said that Gobineau wrote what became the nineteenth century's classic text of racial fear and prejudice, *Essai sur l'inégalité des races humaines,* in order to glorify his own family, to create a superior category of human being to which his own personal 'race' might belong.[21] This presents an ironic genealogy to the post-Holocaust self-deprecation of 'I wouldn't belong to a club that would have me as a member,' a quip attributed to Groucho Marx. The opposite move, setting up of a club so that one might join, involves distancing what has been constructed as an inferior race even (or especially) if that race is one's own. And, as Gilman has illustrated, the best way to do so is to describe the outsider as if he had nothing in common with you.[22]

This is the move that Cesare Lombroso made when describing the problem of antisemitism near the end of the century. When it came time for Lombroso to give his expert opinion on virulent antisemitism, he claimed what he called a scientific impartiality and did not reveal his own Jewish identity in the text. The logical solution to antisemitism, in Lombroso's scientific hands, becomes assimilation, or the complete obliteration of difference and therefore the end of Judaism. In his analysis of what is Jewish, Lombroso's constant subtext becomes the faults of the Jews, and he ends up aligning these purported faults with his analysis of women. What he calls 'impartiality' is ultimately a thin veil for his own prejudices against Jews and women.

Similarly, Matilde Serao, when marshaling her resources against the threat of emancipation for women, decided for the most part to refuse to align or identify herself with other women. A nineteenth-century Italian novelist and journalist, Serao incorporates severely contradictory attitudes toward women both in her novels and her journalistic essays, expressing prejudices against women's suffrage, divorce, and female autonomy outside the home. She utilizes antisemitic stereotypes in some of her novels to address questions of cultural and religious difference. She aligns Jewish and female characters in one of her novels and dramatizes the plight of marginalization while at the same time demonstrating her own frequent incapacity to identify with the economic and social situation of other women.

What antisemitism and misogyny have in common in the nineteenth century are many small points of connection in the dreary landscape of biologically fortified prejudice, connections to be demonstrated in the chapters to come. In their work Lombroso and Serao theorize cultural and religious difference; they also employ strategies in an attempt to contain and control it. These theories and strategies reveal how the discourses of antisemitism and misogyny not only resemble each other but spring from some of the same sources.[23]

What these two authors share are similar ways of reacting to their own marginalization – Lombroso as a Jew, Serao as a woman – that bring a cohesiveness to their texts, an impression that their texts are intimately connected even though their disciplines are different and their textual media quite divergent. Lombroso and Serao employ two important perspectives in their dealings with otherness that intimately link them: first, the way in which they wield the science of their day to theorize the status of disenfranchised groups, and second, their relationship to themselves as members of these highly problematic groups and how that essential conflict is confronted. 'Self-hatred,' a term sometimes applied loosely and broadly, in particular in the context of Jewish self-hatred, is too strong a label for these two authors. Its polemical stance tends to obscure the nuances and complexities of that particular psychological and cultural state that we could refer to more accurately in the cases of Lombroso and Serao as self-obliteration and self-betrayal.

The betrayal of self-identity that is thematized in the works of Lombroso and Serao is related quite essentially to the metaphorization of the quagga as the stigma of uncontrolled and threatening difference. Like most of nineteenth-century racism, this difference is purported to have a biological basis but bears the marks of strong cultural assumptions. The motivations behind the self-erasure advocated explicitly by Lombroso and implicitly by Serao are closely related to the worries about the taint of the quagga so studiously examined by nineteenth-century scientists attempting to 'resolve' the dilemma of heredity. Like the recurring stripes of the quagga that plagued future generations of purportedly 'purebred' Arabians, the issue of cultural difference is not simple to resolve: the stripes do not fade quickly, the 'stigmata' of difference are not easy to obliterate. The following chapters endeavor to demonstrate the strategies these two authors employ in the service of confronting uncomfortable difference.

CHAPTER TWO

THE LOGIC OF INTOLERANCE: LOMBROSO, MODERN SCIENCE, & WOMAN

Cesare Lombroso, Criminologist

Cesare Lombroso is generally considered the greatest prison reformer since Cesare Beccaria.[1] Several of his ideas, such as indeterminate sentencing, parole, and juvenile court, are still widely adopted in the United States.[2] His attempts to standardize an approach to the criminal resulted in his theory of the physical signs of the criminal body.[3] The mind seemed to have little to do with criminal behavior, as the signs of the 'born criminal' were entirely physical. If society could understand the physical as well as the moral dimensions of crime, it could better contain criminal elements.

Along with these innovative ideas came a whole set of categories governing what we might call the management of cultural difference. What is particularly interesting about Lombroso's formulation of difference is his tendency to shift from physical to cultural manifestations. This is particularly apparent in his analysis, interpretation of, and reaction to what he defines as female and as Jewish. As I will demonstrate, the particular scientific methodology that Lombroso employs to study difference ultimately betrays its own subjectivity and reveals his attitudes not only toward the diversity of women and Jews but toward his own difference as well.

Lombroso was born in Turin in 1835 and died in 1909. His

ancestors were immigrants from Spain who settled in the prominent Italian Jewish communities of Florence, Leghorn, and Venice at the end of the fifteenth century. Educated as a doctor, he was primarily interested in psychiatry and anthropometry, and he describes himself in his 1894 text *L'antisemitismo e le scienze moderne* [Antisemitism and Modern Science] as a practitioner of psychiatry and experimental anthropology. Lombroso's training as a doctor is particularly relevant in the mid-nineteenth century,[4] when doctors were aggressively colonizing the social sciences. Their opinions about various aspects of community and family life were invested with much authority as they strove to be considered a kind of scientific and therefore more competent substitution for the local clergy.[5]

During his lifetime and for at least thirty years after his death, Lombroso's theories were taken seriously by scientists and the general public alike. Havelock Ellis, one of the most prominent psychologists in England at the time, acknowledged both his own debt to Lombroso and Lombroso's role in the disciplinary development of criminology in his 1890 book, *The Criminal*: 'If Lombroso has been the Columbus who led the way to a fresh scientific region, let us be grateful; we may take it for granted, without more ado, that any petty surveyor who follows him can more accurately map out the land than its discoverer could.'[6] Leon Radzinowicz writes that 'virtually every element of value in contemporary criminological knowledge owes its formulation to that very remarkable school of Italian criminologists who took pride in describing themselves as the "positivists." '[7] According to Leonard D. Savitz, who wrote the introduction to the most current edition in English translation of *Criminal Man,* not all scholars of criminology would agree with this hyperbolic assessment, but there is nonetheless general consensus that Lombroso and the school of positivist criminology that resulted from his theories had a tremendous impact on the development of the discipline.[8] The French environmentalist school of criminology, which emphasized the role of surroundings rather than biology in the creation of the criminal, was the greatest opponent of Lombrosian theory in Europe but was largely ignored in the United States.[9]

The methods employed by Lombroso for gathering and analyzing material were freely adapted from those of several scientists who preceded him. Of particularly strong influence was the work of Paul Broca, the anthropometrist who developed instruments to measure certain features of the human anatomy. Lombroso's particular contribution to the field of anthropometry was his selection of criminals as a subject of study.

The relationship of Lombroso to his predecessors in the field of criminal anthropology is a complex one, for during his long career the anthropometric method – which enjoyed widespread acceptance in the middle of the century – came under fire and Lombroso himself began to question its validity late in his career. In the preface to what is probably his most problematic work, *La donna delinquente, la prostituta e la donna normale,* [The Criminal Woman, the Prostitute, and the Normal Woman] (1893) his long text coauthored with his son-in-law Guglielmo Ferrero, he makes clear the challenge that the anthropometric method had to face. His own ambivalence toward this method and toward the difficult position in which this methodological crisis had put him comes out as well.

Having determined the essential characteristics of the 'born' male criminal in his landmark 1879 text, *L'uomo delinquente* [Criminal Man], Lombroso turned his attention in the later part of his career to the 'fairer' sex: fairer on the outside, perhaps, but with an atavistic viciousness lying just under the serene surface of idealized nineteenth-century womanhood. In identifying the *criminale nato,* Lombroso did not attempt to define what is particularly 'male' about these criminals, but he did connect criminal behavior with atavistic signs linking the delinquent to a primitive, savage world. When Lombroso concentrates on the female of the criminal species, as it were, the focus of analysis changes as he attempts, both covertly and overtly, to define what is female – as if the question, 'What is female?' was as important as the question, 'What is the female criminal?' In fact, he ultimately conflates these two, making his interpretation of the identity of the prostitute a middle ground to facilitate this move between the identity of woman and that of the female criminal.

Lombroso finally turns his attention to two cultural targets that are really much closer to him than the world of the criminal: women and Jews. His analysis of the latter came just after he completed the work on women: *L'antisemitismo e le scienze moderne* [Antisemitism and Modern Science] was published in 1894, one year after *La donna delinquente, la prostituta e la donna normale*. The choice of subject matter is not surprising, as scientists since Darwin had been trying to understand the place of the female in evolution and racialist science had been studying the Jew in relation to some of the same questions raised by studies of women and blacks. What perhaps *is* surprising is that Lombroso waited so long in his career to study these two groups. As we will see, the correlation of deviancy and what he defines as 'Jewish' and 'female' informs Lombroso's interpretation and analysis of both. Before dealing with the main part of the text, I will examine Lombroso's preface to *La donna delinquente* to illustrate certain methodological problems that underlie his analysis.

Reading the Preface: The Burden of Methodology

On the surface, the preface, written by Lombroso without the collaboration of Guglielmo Ferrero, presents an argument concerning his view of women and the issues he will confront in the book. It serves as well to demonstrate the methodological anxieties that come out as he attempts to elucidate and defend his method. He begins the preface with a statement about scientific methodology and its relation to his current enterprise:

Among the numerous quantities of new research in criminal anthropology, that on the female criminal and the prostitute confirms the advantage of the blind observation of facts more than any other. . . . The major results, in fact, which were obtained from the initial research, stood in opposition to commonly held premises. Even individual, partial observations seemed to contradict themselves; consequently, whoever for love of the system wanted to be logical, had to hesitate before arriving at any definite conclusions.[10]

The 'blind observation of facts' is Lombroso's clarion call for the empirical method the work will ostensibly follow. The contradictions that issue out of his study of women might seem to be a problem, but Lombroso dispatches this difficulty through the following metaphor, found in the next paragraph of the preface:

Faithful to the principles which have sustained us our whole life, we have blindly followed the facts, even when they most seemed to contradict one another, even when they seemed to lead us in the wrong direction. Nor were we mistaken: for when the snare was tightened, the most opposite facts, fitting together like the pieces of a mosaic, formed a complete and organic design. And if the mode of gathering at first seems uncertain and tedious like he who gropes in the dark, when at the end a clear and lucid goal appeared to us, we felt the sharp pleasure of the hunter who snares the prey along cliffs and crags, and his joyous success doubled after the anxiety of defeat and the labors of victory.

These rebounds, like the waves of the sea, frequently carried us away from the established goal. What's even better is that further along they helped us to flatten out the continual contradictions which faced us from the beginning.[11]

This set of mixed metaphors, used to describe the study of women, reveals quite a lot about Lombroso the thinker and scientist. The logic of the passage proceeds as follows: the facts are followed, just as a hunter tracks the prey, and numerous contradictions ignored until the whole picture falls into place. A hypothesis has thus been formed and tested. Even though the metaphors in this passage are mixed, they reflect a common theme, a hunter-prey relationship between the scientist and his facts. Facts are figured like difficult and elusive targets that the hunter-scientist must aggressively track down to the bitter end, resulting in the 'death' of the prey. The surrendering of the fact to the hand of the scientist involves 'a sharp pleasure' for him. The masculinity of these images is as noteworthy as the bloodthirsty image of the scientist, who forces these facts into submission as he ropes them together in a frenzy of intellectual pleasure. Lombroso's use of such strongly masculine imagery to convey the methodological undertaking of the scientist follows an androcentric bias still common in science today.[12] In evaluating what constitutes androcentric bias and what kinds of ramifications it has had in the development of scientific methodology, Evelyn Fox Keller states:

> Such an inversion of the personal and impersonal constitutes a far more radical, and correspondingly more problematic, challenge to traditional conceptions of objectivity than that initiated by recent historians and sociologists of science. It suggests that our 'laws of nature' are more than simple expressions of the results of objective inquiry or of political and social pressures: they must also be read for their personal – and by tradition, masculine – content. It uncovers, in short, the personal investment scientists make in impersonality; the anonymity of the picture they produce is revealed as itself a kind of signature.[13]

Lombroso's imagery in his preface and his statements about objectivity and impartiality demonstrate the kind of situation Keller describes and also goes beyond it: while he is anxious about objectivity, his analysis of the role of the scientist reveals at the same time how partial the scientific enterprise can be. His signature is doubly inscribed as claiming impartiality while revealing a clear itinerary.

In the passage cited, the strong hand of the scientist is

apparent in the description of what ultimately happens to contradictions: they are flattened in this process of snaring and taming. The mixed nature of the images themselves bears closer examination. The passage begins with the 'tracking' of the facts, then suddenly shifts to a snare. The snare gives way to the image of a mosaic within which the facts could or should fit. This sudden shift from hunterly images to artistic ones raises the question of a paranomastic moment in the text. 'Mosaico' [Eng. mosaic] is probably not etymologically related to the adjective signifying something attributable to Moses, *mosaico* [Eng. Mosaic], but it is certainly linked verbally and visually. In what seems to be a gratuitous shift of metaphor, Lombroso has evoked, wittingly or not, the name of Moses, lawgiver, as the figure for the trap for his elusive facts. Yet, as if dissatisfied with this new metaphor, Lombroso changes images once again, this time to a confused groping in the dark. The success of the hunter, after this initial confusion, joyously awaits him 'along cliffs and crags.' The scene has shifted dramatically from confusion and uncertainty to triumph. The movement of these changing images and metaphors for the hunt for facts is centered around tension generated by a 'mosaic' appreciation of the difficulties of arriving at the truth.

Some questions need to be asked of this text: Which facts are being followed – how are they chosen? – and what is the role of the contradictions in either denying or affirming preliminary conclusions drawn along the way? In other words, how is the itinerary of the hunt set up if not through preconceived notions, notions that are expressed, for example, through the questions being asked or the facts that are selected? Of course the idea that the question itself at least in part presupposes the answer is now a commonplace in the epistemology of science, but in Lombroso's time the metaphor of the hunt supported the idea of how science discovers new ideas. The arbitrary nature of the hunt as Lombroso describes it is quite close to the epistemological category of abduction, systematized philosophically by Charles Sanders Peirce at the end of the century but current long before then.[14] Lombroso would no doubt have been aware of the work of Claude Bernard, the French physician who in 1861 wrote the *Introduction to Experimental Medicine*. The method described by Bernard is precisely that of abduction, as he theorizes about the way in which the scientist comes across a surprising fact, works retroactively to establish the reasons for its presence, and finally comes up with a hypothesis that explains it.[15]

As Renzo Villa has pointed out in the introduction to his study of Lombroso, 'And this [criminology] did not develop out of nothing: several decades before Lombroso's chief work of 1876, *Criminal Man,* criminals and deviants were already objects of study and research. And yet the panorama of the "human sciences" of the last century would seem in some way nebulous without that work and its influence. So it is a question of following – rereading and reconstructing – an itinerary which is cultural, and, for its time, scientific.'[16]

In his assessment of the particular kind of itinerary that he sees in Lombroso's work, Villa alludes to a complex set of problems that tends to accompany any study of the cultural or scientific content of nineteenth-century science. What is particularly clear is that the 'itinerary' Villa refers to can easily become an ideological one on the part of the scholar who projects a kind of snobbish relativism while laying claim to a cultural or scientific superiority. We see more than a hint of this in Steven Jay Gould's assessment of Lombroso: 'Lombroso constructed virtually all his arguments in a manner that precluded their defeat, thus making them scientifically vacuous. He cited copious numerical data to lend an air of objectivity to his work, but it remained so vulnerable that even most of Broca's school turned against [him]. Whenever Lombroso encountered a contrary fact, he performed some mental gymnastics to incorporate it within his system.'[17]

Gould's view is both helpful and limited. Lombroso's manipulation of facts is indeed clear to the modern reader, but

Gould's analysis is ultimately reductive because the complexities and nuances that inform Lombroso's method are not taken into account but rather grouped together by Gould under the rubric of 'incorrect,' or, as he puts it, 'scientifically vacuous.' However justified Gould's scientific appraisal of Lombroso, it does not attempt to locate Lombroso in the context of nineteenth-century scientific epistemology. Gould's characterization of Lombroso's method as 'vacuous' may be correct, but it fails to consider just how much Lombroso's method reveals about the subject matter it engages. Lombroso's preface is a text that takes on, either overtly or covertly, some of the most pressing scientific and cultural concerns of the late nineteenth century – for example, the place and identity of women in society and the role of science as the discipline that can potentially explain and mediate important social issues through the application of scientific methodology. The issues raised in the preface are relevant both to that time and to present-day versions of intimately related concerns.[18]

I would like to make two further comments regarding a methodological critique of Lombroso. There are noteworthy differences between Lombroso's early and later work in respect to the anthropometric method that he initially embraced wholeheartedly and about which he later became more skeptical. I do not intend here to settle the debate, still current in the history of science, as to whether the entire work of many nineteenth-century scientists must be dismissed because of flawed methods of measuring and interpreting their data. I am instead more concerned with the cultural bias that Lombroso demonstrates in his work concerning women and Jews and the way in which he attempts to work out the discrepancies – the contradictions, as he calls them – he encounters in his attempts to categorize the difference of women and Jews. Methodology, as we will see, is a vehicle for this bias and is for that reason important whether it works or not in any objective sense.

The assessments he makes of women and of Jews are invariably from this later period, in which his own methodology is called into question and becomes a point of crisis. This crisis is generated not only by Lombroso's contemporaries, his opponents in the French environmentalist school who saw the flaws of anthropometry. More interesting, in fact, it is generated by Lombroso himself. This methodological questioning becomes internal to Lombroso's work, and it exceeds the bounds of the viability of anthropometry. It is my contention that it specifically appears in his work on women because of the tension created by this choice of subject matter and his own ambivalence and antagonism toward them.

A close reading of Lombroso's preface tells us not only that his reasoning is contrived to support his beliefs, as Gould suggests, but that he himself demonstrates a level of anxiety regarding this problem, as illustrated by his emphasis on method (the 'blind following of facts' is repeated twice in the first two paragraphs) and the long, elaborate metaphor regarding the pulling in of contradictions and the usefulness of the enterprise. 'Contrary facts,' as Gould calls them, are clearly central to Lombroso's method, the 'pieces of a mosaic,' in his words. These facts might more accurately be called the *product* of his method.

Lombroso goes on to repeat some of the post-Darwinian beliefs among scientists regarding woman and her status: 'We saw the female in the lowest zoological order superior to the male in size, sophistication of organs, almost mistress of the species, then fall to become a humble slave, reduced in strength, in variability, etc. And so in our race she appears equal or superior to man before puberty in strength and size, often in intelligence, but then slowly falls behind, leaving in that same momentary superiority a proof of the precocity which is typical of the inferior races.'[19]

The sentiment that 'precocity' is common to the lower races is part of the theory of recapitulation, 'ontogeny recapitulates phylogeny,' that was first developed by Ernst Haeckel, a Dar-

winian from Germany. Cynthia Eagle Russett, in her study
Sexual Science: The Victorian Construction of Womanhood,
defines this theory in the following way: 'In its simplest form
the concept of recapitulation asserts that every individual or-
ganism repeats in its own life history the life history of its race,
passing through the lower forms of its ancestors on its way to
maturity.'[20] The basic theme of recapitulation is that 'lower'
groups or races would get stuck somewhere on this ladder of
development, at first showing signs of precocity and then ar-
rested development. This part of the concept was used to explain away any superiority that women and non-Caucasians
might show as children. In fact, any precociousness was then
presented as proof of their eventual inferiority. Russett explains why this theory was so attractive to scientists at the
time: 'Recapitulation theory proved irresistible to the social
sciences. It provided a program for greater anthropological
understanding of all those groups outside the charmed circle
of Caucasian male adulthood – children, women, and the
lower races. In so doing it became the thematic core of anthropology, of psychology, and of child study. That women, children and savages shared many traits in common was a finding
that appeared to emerge from the evidence of physical anthro-
pologists and psychologists. Recapitulation shed light on why
this might be so.'[21]

In his discussion of the measurement of bodies, Gould tells
us of the importance and the influence of recapitulation: 'Both
Sigmund Freud and C. G. Jung were convinced recapitula-
tionists, and Haeckel's idea played no small role in the development of psychoanalytic theory. . . . Recapitulation served
as a general theory of biological determinism. All inferior
groups – races, sexes, and classes – were compared with the
children of white males.'[22] It is important to add the adjective 'Christian' to the 'children of white males,' since non-
Christians were largely outsiders to the nineteenth-century
European society that produced the scientists and their theories of recapitulation.[23]

Returning to Lombroso's preface, we see that the figure of the woman who is defined as a 'humble slave' creates a moment of tension even within the contradictory frame of this work, as Lombroso toward the end of the preface acknowledges the difficulty of reconciling misogyny with the enterprise of actually living with women in the world:

> How much woman can be useful and dear to us, these noted ladies Mrs. Caccia, Dr. Tarnowsky, Miss Helen Zimmern, Mrs. C. Royer, Mrs. Rossi, Dr. Kulischioff have well proved in this book as they understood my ideas better, earlier, and more extensively than many of our thinkers. They have collaborated in this study with documents, stories, and advice in the most difficult areas. You, my dearest Gina, prove this more than anyone, the last and only link which ties me to this life, my collaborator and inspiration, more steadfast and fecund than any of my works.[24]

Is Lombroso trying to have it both ways here? His lauding of women ('how much woman can be useful and dear to us') is 'proven' by the fact that the women he names here have understood his ideas better than have many others. So what makes these women useful to the author is their ability not only to comprehend his work but to collaborate in it as well. They are both 'inferior,' as his theories demonstrate, and 'superior,' as they are able to understand these same theories. They collaborate in two ways: they have helped in the gathering of information and are also cited in the preface as supporting the theories, thereby furthering them. They therefore simultaneously prove them wrong and perpetuate them through such collaboration.

How can Lombroso reconcile his beliefs about women's inferiority, capacity for cruelty, underlying immorality, and other negative characteristics with his liberal and socialist outlook? The question of the role of liberalism and its theories of Jewish assimilation will be discussed in the next chapter in light of Lombroso's views on Jews. For the time being I will limit this broad question to an attempt to establish the contradictory nature of virtually all the social, political, religious, and scientific ideas that emerge in Lombroso's work about marginalized groups that are close to him. The question that must accompany that regarding his personal and political attitudes is how the women he names, including the famous feminist Anna Kulischioff, could have accepted his theories to the point of collaborating in the collection of 'proofs' regarding their validity. I will take this up in the chapters to come, both in relation to the acceptability of Otto Weininger's theories for the generation of writers and thinkers just after his death in 1903 and in relation to Matilde Serao, whose work also expresses great ambivalence about marginality while simultaneously revealing strategies for coping with it.[25]

What we see in examining Lombroso's preface is a melange of what would appear to be essentially contradictory attitudes, reflected in the hodgepodge of 'contrary facts' that he finds in his research. The pressure created from these divergent points of view comes out in the following passage:

> Those who in the books on women don't content themselves with the ironclad logic of facts, but who, continuing or even falsifying medieval traditions, also want chivalry toward the gentle sex who most decorates our life, will find that we have often shown a lack of respect toward woman in our work. But if we didn't respect our most cherished preconceptions, such as the idea of the type, the born criminal, if we weren't afraid of the apparent contradiction that to the inexperienced eye could seem deleterious to our work as a whole, how could we have passively followed a conventional lie, not at all scientific, that acquires a form only to lose it immediately?[26]

Once again we are met with the 'ironclad logic of facts,' a logic that is locked tight, closed. It is the blunt presence of facts that leads to such immobility on the part of logic: facts guide logic, yet close it up at the same time. The expression that Lombroso uses here demonstrates the security of the empirical method, a system in which facts and logic join together to present an impenetrable fortress.

Lombroso sets up chivalry as an oppositional term to what he has 'discovered' about the nature of women. Chivalry, with its elegiac attitude toward women, has covered up the lie about what they are really like, the 'conventional lie' that Lombroso refers to here. This 'conventional lie' about the nature of women is not scientific; in fact, it is presented here as the opposite of science and thus is unable to explain the enigma of woman to either the scientific community or anyone else. Lombroso seems to be commenting as well on the nature of conventional beliefs and their transmission in culture, since he says at the end of the passage that the conventional lie takes on a form only to lose it, in other words, to mutate in some way. This *methodological* statement regarding what will or will not work in analyzing women will take on more significance as we examine the method that Lombroso actually employs in his text to arrive at his theories regarding the nature of woman. What he uses as 'facts' – these same facts that guide and ultimately control logic – are most telling and eventually put his system into crisis.

So what method is scientific and sufficiently empirical to satisfy Lombroso the measuring scientist? Certainly not anthropometry, which has come under attack and which Lombroso half criticizes, half defends: 'But one must not abandon those measurements, even if they are only the frame of the picture, like a symbol, like a flag of a school, that makes numbers its best weapon. All the more so in those few times when an anomaly is discovered: its importance is doubled.' Thirty years earlier he had believed fully in anthropometry, but now he does not.[27] Yet Lombroso continues to use measurements to back up his points. What is abundantly clear, however, is that he depends more on already-established cultural beliefs than on any other single mode: for example, he cites proverbs, literature, and the sayings of other 'experts' before him, whose 'proofs' he neither reproduces for the benefit of the reader nor even challenges, as long as they concur with his views. Lombroso's attitude toward the subject is thus corroborated by 'group' beliefs. This dependence on beliefs, stereotypes, and so on is particularly noteworthy, given Lombroso's remarks regarding the unreliability of chivalric traditions.

Hearsay evidence forms another kind of source for the text, as he tells us when he thanks that list of *signore* who collaborated 'with documents, stories, and advice in the most difficult areas.' For example, in a passage concerning the psychology of women, in order to 'prove' his point regarding the reasons 'normal' women desire men, he cites an obstetrician who said to him, 'Man loves woman for her vulva, woman loves man for his being a husband and father.'[28] This statement demonstrates more than Lombroso's tendency to convert cliché into evidence. A crude sentiment, it shows as well a reductive view of woman as valuable only for her sexual service. At the same time, it figures man as a simplistic creature who would stoop to such a banality and makes woman seem exploitative of man as well (in his role as a husband and father). This sentiment is presented as if, by virtue of its being said, it automatically constitutes proof. Ultimately, though, it cuts both ways in its show of ambivalence about the role of the sexes.

As we have seen, Lombroso incorporates the use of contradiction in his method. What is puzzling is a major contradiction of another kind that exists alongside the *methodological* use of contradiction explained above. The following statement from the preface makes the point:

> Consequently, not a single line of this work justifies the many tyrannies to which women have been and are still subjected: from the taboos that prohibit them from eating meat or touching coconut to those that impede them from learning or, what's worse, practicing a profession once it has been learned. These are ridiculous or cruel coercions, always arrogant, with which we have helped to maintain, and what's even sadder, increase woman's inferiority, in order to exploit her to our advantage, for example when we hypocritically heaped the docile victim with praise in which we

did not believe. Rather than a decoration, this is a preparation for new sacrifices.[29]

The analysis of the relationship of flattery and praise to the subservience of women is surprising here and, moreover, indicative of Lombroso's liberal politics, which themselves seem to exude contradiction.[30] While he believes in the inherent inferiority of women, Lombroso is willing to acknowledge the role of men in worsening this condition and in exploiting it. Any analysis of Lombroso's views toward women needs for the sake of balance to account for his attitude toward his own sex, an ambivalence that is apparent in the two examples cited above.

Women, Love, and Blood: The Untouchables

Lombroso's agenda in *La donna delinquente* is not only to isolate and characterize the female criminal but to analyze what is female, as he returns obsessively to the definition of the 'normal' woman and her not-so-aberrational counterpart, the criminal or prostitute. Just what *is* female for Lombroso, in the 'normative' sense he sets out to establish, is demonstrated in the last section of this long text. Although Lombroso coauthored this text with his son-in-law, the young historian Guglielmo Ferrero, Lombroso was the senior author who had ultimate responsibility, and he alone wrote the preface. The text was only partially translated into English, under the title *The Female Offender*, a weak effort not only in its rendition of the title – 'female offender' is after all a rather genteel version of 'woman criminal' – but also in the omission of almost all of the material concerning prostitutes and all that dealt with the 'normal' woman. What was not understood by the unnamed translator was that, for Lombroso, the three terms *woman criminal, prostitute,* and *woman* were inseparable. The theory of their inseparability is explicated by Lombroso over and over again in his text. '*La donna delinquente,*' or criminal woman, indicates the point of departure of the study; what happens when the female criminal is studied is that her two sisters, the prostitute and the normal woman, become unmasked as well.

According to Lombroso, lower-class women are closer to nature and thus more prone to criminal behavior, whereas bourgeois women are more cultured and farther from nature, more liable to be 'healthy' and 'normal.'[31] In his categorical refusal to assign much importance to the effect of environment, Lombroso's work is in line with other scientific theorists of the nineteenth century, yet this produces an internal inconsistency – one of many – within his thought. If environment is of little or no importance, how does social class play a role in Lombroso's ideas regarding who becomes a criminal and for what reason? This inconsistency is another signpost to the cultural nature of Lombroso's analysis, which purports to depend entirely on physical manifestations in the criminal.

Lombroso's view of woman as essentially criminal and immoral is clear. He refers, for example, to 'that latent base of immorality that is found in every woman,' as well as 'that latent base of evil that is found in every woman.'[32] He continues: 'It is clear that from that innocuous semicriminaloid that is the normal woman, a born-criminal would emerge who is more terrible than any male delinquent. What fierce criminals children would be if they had great passions, strength, and intelligence and if furthermore their tendency toward evil were exacerbated by a sick excitation! Women are like big children: their tendencies toward evil are more numerous and varied than in man, just that they remain almost always latent. When, however, they are activated and reawakened, the result is of course much greater.'[33] Like some other nineteenth-century scientists, Lombroso believed that women had much in common with children. They lie 'naturally,' he says, as if it were an integral part of their natures. At the beginning of the section entitled 'Lie' of *La donna delinquente* Lombroso tells us, 'To show that the lie is habitual and almost physiological to women would be superfluous because it is so widespread in popular legend.' He then lists ten proverbs, such as 'women always say the truth, but never in its entirety' and 'women – says Dohm – use lies like the bull uses his horns.'[34] He follows up these sayings with citations from Flaubert, Schopenhauer, Zola, Molière, and Stendhal, all claiming the purported propensity of women to untruth. There is no distinction made between quotations from literary creations of these authors and direct statements from the authors themselves. Lombroso's use of such cultural expressions to make a 'scientific' point is the most unscientific part of his method, revealing an irrefutable link between the cultural prejudices he draws on as 'evidence' and his own bias.

Woman's salvation, and, at the same time, her damnation, is physiology: 'Maternity is, we would almost say, itself a moral vaccination against crime and evil.'[35] Maternity, and also culture and bourgeois society, usually keeps the criminal tendencies in women at bay. For the male, culture is his product, and thus the male criminal, criminal behavior, immorality, and so on are atavistic throwbacks. The 'normal' male has no connection to atavism, whereas the male criminal is not ultimately responsible for his condition because of its sheer force. Women, on the other hand, are all potential criminals, and only the restraining forces of culture and their maternal physiology may – or, of course, may *not* (the real fear here) – keep this criminality suppressed. In analyzing Lombroso's ideas, it is important to keep in mind that Lombroso tells us that there are many male criminals, very few female criminals (i.e., those who have committed murder, arson, theft, etc. on a regular basis), and many female prostitutes. Lombroso's definition of male criminality comprises acts such as theft, arson, and murder. Female criminality can also be expressed through these more 'male' forms of behavior, but the underlying motivation is nonetheless their sexuality. Lombroso makes it clear that the most typical female 'crime' is prostitution. The idea that prostitution is criminal behavior is, of course, problematic, but the fact that Lombroso views it as unequivocally so, and that in his analysis prostitution is the female version of crime and all women are latent criminals, makes it likely that it is really women's sexuality that is on trial.[36]

Women are continually described by Lombroso as 'closer to nature' than men: more atavistic, nearer to their primeval ancestor, the female savage. The strongly sexual nature of primitive woman provides another link to her modern relative, since 'if primitive woman was only rarely an assassin, she was, as we have proved above . . . always a prostitute, and remained thus almost up until the semi-civilized epoch; so even atavistically one can explain that the prostitute must have more regressive traits than the female criminal.' He further characterizes primitive woman as a type: 'The prostitute reproduces more atavistically the primitive woman, the fair Venus.'[37]

An understanding of the prostitute helps us to understand the 'normal' woman, and Lombroso goes to great lengths to explain both his conception of the prostitute and the history of prostitution, since he claims that this history will illuminate the nature of modern women. An important aspect of prostitutes is their virility, which is precisely what, in Lombroso's analysis, makes them less female. Certain physical characteristics indicate their virility: for example, the masculine larynx, 'one would say the larynx of a man. And thus in the larynx, as well as the face and the cranium, the characteristics particular to them comes out: virility.' He notes, as well, the 'virile distribution of hair' found in many prostitutes.[38] He then offers a theory of the mutability of the characteristics of the young prostitute as she ages:

> Even in the most beautiful criminals, however, their virile aspect – the exaggeration of the jaw, the cheekbones – is never missing, just as it is never missing in any of our great courtesans. Thus they all have a familial look which links the Russian sinners to those who pound the streets, whether they be in gilded carriages or humble rags. When youth disappears, those jaws and plump rounded cheeks give way to prominent angles and makes the face completely virile, ug-

33

lier than a man. Wrinkles deepen like a wound, and that once pleasing face shows the degenerate type which youth had hidden.[39]

We see in this description a discursive shift from a 'scientific' mode of observation ('the exaggeration of the jaw, the cheekbones') to a more poetic one ('wrinkles deepen like a wound'). This shift ultimately ends in delusion: the image of the beautiful woman turns out to be a facade for an ugly, wrinkled hag – a virile one in this case – lying just underneath the surface of youth. The underlying notion is that of the woman as trickster and as falsification personified as she seduces her client through her youthful appearance that hides the 'man' underneath. The idea that a certain type of woman is really a man under the surface is compounded by the fact that she sells what is supposed to be specifically female sex to her male clients. That Lombroso is suggesting that she is not really female at all casts an even more onerous light on the situation. What is being sold is pure artifice, then: not female, thus not female sex, but rather a kind of androgynous, ultimately falsified and fraudulent substitution.

The contradiction in Lombroso's analysis of the prostitute is obvious – the 'normal' woman is closer to nature, in other words, more atavistic, than man. Primitive woman, he states, equals prostitution. Yet the prostitute is figured as virile. So what is less female is at the same time more female: more atavistic, that is, more prostitute; more prostitute, less female.

Woman is most 'female' during her menstrual period, according to Lombroso. Hilde Olrik sees a connection here between 'heredity, sexuality, and menstrual blood.'[40] She then discusses briefly the role of cultural taboos regarding menstruation in Lombroso's thought. Lombroso's Judaism (which Olrik does not mention) is certainly pertinent to his culturally conditioned views regarding menstrual blood.

The history of prohibitions and taboos regarding women's blood is a long and complex one with many episodes, as Janice Delaney, Mary Jane Lupton, and Emily Toth document.[41]

Their discussion of menstrual taboos in Judaism and Christianity cites the laws regarding menstruation that are found in Leviticus: 'The position of women in all the books of the Bible, both Old and New Testaments, depends upon these rules in Leviticus. . . . [T]he practices of the early Hebrews parallel the taboos and practices of many of the other early societies we have mentioned. The difference is that Judaism has never abolished the taboos; even today, an Orthodox Jewish woman is required to abstain from sex until seven days after her period has ended and after she has immersed herself in the mikveh, or ritual bath.'[42]

In Judaism, women's blood is something that sets them apart and requires their segregation for a prescribed amount of time during each menstrual cycle.[43] The laws of *niddah* [uncleanliness] have been strictly adhered to for thousands of years by observant Jews, and Lombroso certainly would have been aware of these laws. This is particularly pertinent given his view of menstruation as the most essential female state. If what is most female simultaneously signals that which is taboo and which requires segregation, then it seems clear that the formula 'more female, more to be avoided' emerges from this logic.

After numerous citations regarding women from other authors and sources, Lombroso's voice is finally heard, as he says, 'And about lies women have no shame; they say them without blushing, the most spirited of them use them with absolute confidence for pious ends.'[44] There is no critical distance between the proverbs Lombroso cites, the cultural voices that he quotes, and his own opinions and conclusions regarding women and lying. At a certain point in his argument – or, rather, his pastiche of borrowed arguments – Lombroso states that 'in many languages the word *swear, testimony,* is connected with testicle (for example, Latin *testis*).'[45] Telling the truth, 'testimony,' is quite literally *not* a part of women's physiology, since it is testicular. One must be physiologically equipped to tell the truth. Lombroso has already laid the groundwork for this idea in the first sentence of the section, in which he says that the opposite of testimony, lying, is 'almost physiological' to women. He further stresses the link between maleness and testimony, as he gives examples of cultures in which women's testimony is not allowed or where it is held in little regard.

But it is when Lombroso connects menstruation to lying that a certain sympathy for the female condition begins to emerge from the text: 'When menstruation became an object of repulsion for men, woman had to hide it. Even today this is the first lie that is taught to woman. She is conditioned to hide her state with the simulation of other ills. Now this means that woman is constrained to lie continuously for two or three days every month, this is to say an exercise in periodic dissimulation.'[46]

He links this condition to *pudore,* a word whose definition falls between 'modesty' and 'shame,' and cites Stendhal: 'Modesty – writes Stendhal – has this disadvantage, that it habituates one to lie.'[47] Lombroso continues: 'And if modesty comes from *putere* – to stink – one sees how from the beginning of time one had to get used to lies.'[48] There is a sudden shift of tone here: Lombroso makes it clear that women are constrained to lie about menstruation because of male attitudes toward it, that they are taught to lie as a matter of necessity. Lombroso's theory regarding *pudore* is that it is – or should be – related to *putere* [to stink]. He claims this connection between *pudore* and *putere* has come about because of a primitive lack of hygiene regarding menstruation. Lombroso's etymologies reveal both what is linguistically connected and what he thinks *should* be connected.

The argument is extended even further with an analysis of how makeup and the artifices of beauty are in themselves little lies. He ends the section with the following statement: 'Women are, in conclusion, big children, and children are the best liars. Women lie so much more easily that the reasons for lying are for them more numerous than for children.'[49] This argument appears to be circular: because women lie more easily, they must have more reasons for doing so than do children. The comparison of women to children in order to point out the shortcomings of the former, of course, is part of recapitulationist theory. It also had been part of a tradition of writing about women that denigrated their intellectual and moral capacities before recapitulation appropriated the idea.

According to Lombroso, women are not only morally deficient but revengeful and jealous as well. He tells long and detailed horror stories of women criminals and their atrocious acts – dismemberment, bodily mutilation, poisoning of husbands and children – to show that, when women are bad, they are very, very bad: much worse, in fact, than their male counterparts.

There is an important factor that can cause criminal behavior in some women and makes their behavior 'not really' their fault: the effect of love and passion on the female. Lombroso declares that, for some women, the force of love is such that they become a slave to it and then will commit any act under its influence. 'Love,' as Lombroso defines it in this chapter, is the emotion felt for an individual man, and it produces a particular effect on the individual woman. Not every woman is susceptible to the out-of-control type of emotion that Lombroso describes, and he is unable to categorize these women through physical signs or even through a more generalized concept of women's 'nature.' There is a problematic separation between sexuality, which is a strong determinant for a thinker like Lombroso, and 'love,' which causes a kind of craziness that is not connected either to atavism or to women's 'nature.' The effects of love and passion succeed in transcending Lombroso's definition of female sexuality.

In his discussion of women criminals, Lombroso also points out their shortcomings and excesses in the area of language: 'And one understands how chattering about the crime is more frequent in the woman than in the man, because she must supplement all those means that the male has to revivify the image of the crime, like drawings and writing, that we see lacking in the woman. The woman speaks often of her crimes, just like the man draws them, writes about them, or sculpts them in vases, etc.'[50]

Women criminals, in Lombroso's appraisal, talk too much and write too little. His choice of a word to signify women's talking about crime, the pejorative term *chiacchiera* [chatter], conveys the stereotypically derogatory notion of women's speech. He implies here that women criminals take crime so lightly that they 'chatter' about it. Elsewhere he tells us that women lack the skills and development in 'the graphic area' of the brain, which would explain their reluctance or inability to write at a sophisticated level.[51] He informs us also that women criminals literally cannot keep their mouths shut about their crimes, that they are compelled to tell others and even brag about them. At the same time, they will persevere in the most audacious untruths, even when confronted with absolute proof of the ridiculousness of the lie. Lombroso concludes from all this that women have a poor sense of truth, that they are estranged from reality in some essential way.

Lombroso's pinpointing of language as a locus of attack is significant in that language is often in the discourse of bigotry exactly that part of the culture of difference that is singled out as particularly threatening. Sander Gilman poses this issue in the following terms: 'Language, therefore, in codified systems of representation, traps the outsider as the source of our potential loss of power. This language is ubiquitous. When those who are labeled as marginal are forced to function within the same discourse as that which labels them as different, conflict arises that may not be consciously noted by outsiders, for they are forced to speak using the polluted language that designates them as Other.'[52]

Lombroso's charge that women lie, are unreliable and underdeveloped linguistically, and do not distinguish between truth and untruth thus fits into a more general attack. If the *language* of difference can be made out as entirely unreliable, then it proves in some way that it is in fact the difference itself that is unreliable, threatening, and unstable: not part of main-stream culture, not acceptable because of the danger of the unknown that it poses. Gilman's landmark study of antisemi-tism and the role that language plays in the establishment of categories of intolerance demonstrates this last point.

This review of Lombroso's positions on women, their link to female 'savage' ancestors, and the role of atavism in deter-mining modern woman's alleged propensity to prostitution and crime demonstrates the logic of his method. The role that preconceived ideas and cultural conditioning play in estab-lishing the kinds of questions that he asks and his way of answering them is clear both from his examples and his rea-soning. Thus, an examination of methodology, as it unmasks these structures, is particularly important for an understand-ing of Lombroso's work. The next chapter will examine Lom-broso's text on Jews, *L'antisemitismo e le scienze moderne* [Antisemitism and modern science] in light of what he has theorized about women, look at what happens when his anal-yses of women and Jews converge, in a memorable moment in Lombroso's work, and consider as well some issues in the transmission of his theories regarding women and Jews through the pre-Fascist period.

VILIFYING DIFFERENCE: LOMBROSO AND THE JEWS

L ombroso's classification of the differences of marginalized groups was not limited to women and criminals. In 1894, one year after the appearance of *La donna delinquente,* Lombroso published *L'antisemitismo e le scienze moderne,* an attempt to establish a relationship of scientific impartiality toward a subject about which he was anything but impartial. This text discloses as well certain correlations between women and Jews that are apparent in his thought.

Lombroso informs us in the preface to the book that the work was not necessarily his idea: he was called on by two publications, the *Neue Freie Presse* and *Revue des Revues,* to write a text on the problem of antisemitism. As the originator of the atavistic theory of the criminal, viewed as an exciting new development in criminology, Lombroso was thought to be the one to challenge the theoreticians of antisemitism on their scientific methodologies and overall merit. Lombroso answered these requests with an ostensible defense of the Jews against the biologically based racism developing at the time. From a modern point of view, *L'antisemitismo e le scienze moderne* is not an apologia; rather, it is a thinly shrouded pretext for attack on different grounds than the ones used by racialist theorists, as I will demonstrate.

Lombroso begins his study with an explanation of its origin – the requests he received to write it and the investigative urge that spurred him on: 'I felt that disgust which strikes even the least impatient scientist when he has to study the most revolting human secretions. Deciding whether hatred between peoples can be justified, in our times, is certainly a detestable and sad enterprise, and it is not easy to get used to it.'[1] Lombroso insists in this introduction that the new methods of psychiatry and experimental anthropology, and his own new method of scientific inquiry, would make this investigation an entirely unbiased one: 'This safeguarded me against the perils of partiality, so great in matters like this.' Later in the preface, after listing some of the material and authors he has consulted to help him in this study, he says, 'The help of such assorted experts risen from the nations richest with antisemites and with philosemites was a token to me of the rectitude and the impartiality of my judgment for he who doubts the instrument which I have handled for a short period of time.'[2] Clinging to his role as dispassionate scientist, Lombroso does not mention that he himself is Jewish. We see nonetheless three points of anxiety thus far that would seem to be related to this fact: his concern over justifying antisemitism, his worrying about impartiality, and his self-justification as a competent author of such a study. Similar claims are not made, for example, in his book on women, even though that analysis would seem to warrant corresponding concerns. The emphasis on impartiality can be read as the prevailing ideology of scientific methods and a claim to authority over the material. It can further be interpreted as an expression of Lombroso's anxiety that he is, perhaps, too close to his subject matter.

The text is divided into short chapters that discuss various aspects of antisemitism. The first, entitled 'Cause,' attempts to analyze the phenomenon of intolerance in general. Lombroso believes that intolerance is caused by two principal factors. The first is the satisfaction of a superiority complex, which necessitates the creation of an inferior group. The second has to do with historical memory and its relation to prejudice, which he calls the layering of memory, in which intolerance is passed down from generation to generation and seems to have an almost self-sustaining movement. He discusses the historical development of antisemitism, from Roman times to the medieval period, in which antisemitism became the province of the clergy and thus part of the Christian religious structure. At the end of this short historical sketch Lombroso tacks on some reasons for antisemitism that he directly attributes to the different nature of the Jewish community itself: 'segregation of habitation, the dissonance of customs, food, languages, and competition in business which breeds jealousy, increases real and apparent disparities, making their vilification desirable and useful to individuals and even the state; finally the psychic epidemic which diffuses and amplifies hate and legends.'[3]

A metaleptic argument is present in this passage as Lombroso takes the effect of prejudice as its cause. Vilifying religious and cultural difference, he sets the stage for blaming the victim and in so doing leads us into his next chapter, entitled 'Difetti degli ebrei' [Defects of the Jews]. Opening with the statement 'certainly the character of those persecuted contributed to the persecution,' Lombroso continues to attack the targets of prejudice for their own condition.[4] He goes on to explain how these particular traits and cultural customs of the Jews have abetted prejudice against them. Lying and cleverness are mentioned immediately as two of the defects he singles out. Lombroso's focus on lying brings to mind the same critique he has made of women and their relationship to truth telling. The figure of the Jew that Lombroso draws in this chapter is similar to the stereotypes used by many antisemitic theorists: the Jew as cheating merchant, a dual personality, capable of chameleon-like changes as the situation requires.[5]

The target of Lombroso's attack in this text is what we might call the singularity of the Jews: those customary practices that mark their distinction from the rest of Christian society. He singles out the use of Passover matzoh, the wearing of tefillin [phylacteries], and circumcision. Passover matzoh comes under fire precisely because it *is* a mark of difference, and Lombroso is quite clear on this point: 'The stupid ritual of Passover matzoh, . . . since it differs from usage among the local people, naturally arouses ridicule and revulsion which grows due to the exaggerated importance which the Orthodox attach to it.'[6]

What is particularly interesting about Lombroso's text is the logic of what constitutes difference and how that difference is analyzed and interpreted. The arguments he gives challenging the use of tefillin are especially revealing:

> The custom of tying pieces of leather containing religious formulas to the arm and head (for example, God Is One) goes back certainly to the epoch in which the written word, just invented, assumed among the majority a marvelous importance, a symbolic significance, mystical, so that one almost believed that a written formula could produce miracles. Now that even doormen read thousands of lines a day in the newspapers, to claim that a written formula is magic makes us laugh, or awakens the idea of sad mysteries. The worst part is that this goes even further: the true Orthodox Jew (fortunately there are few of them) arrives at something even stranger, wearing embroidery on his prayer shawl, leftovers from those real *quippu* or mnemonic knots of thread which primitive men had, Peruvians for example, before ideographic writing, before the picture alphabet.[7]

According to Jewish religious practice the tefillin are worn by observant men during morning prayers. They contain parchments of the Torah that hold specific prayers and commandments. In themselves they include the commandment to wear the tefillin. It is not principally the idea of the written word that is being glorified or revered here, it is instead an injunction to remember the commandments to follow religious principles. The physical object serves as a mnemonic device, and the language contained therein refers to *what* it says, not to *that* it says. And the use of tefillin confronts the perception of difference on both counts: the tefillin are a visual mnemonic device that represents linguistic otherness.[8] The idea that 'written formulas could produce miracles' and that they are 'magic' is a figment of Lombroso's imagination and his own skewed interpretation of Judaism.

Lombroso points to a specifically linguistic target, revealing language as that which signifies difference. He connected women's purported lack of writing with a hypothetical graphic underdevelopment in the brain, as I discussed in the last chapter, and suggested that their overuse of verbal language was somehow inappropriate and demonstrated a lack of seriousness. Here, by contrast, it is written language used inappropriately by the Jews that becomes the target of attack. We see that the actual medium of language, whether written or verbal, makes no difference; it is rather the interpretation of the intent (i.e., inappropriate, mystical or magical) and origin (atavistic or underdevelopment) of that medium that creates the discourse of difference. Once difference is established through this logic, the status of 'aberration' that Lombroso assigns it is not far behind.

He uses his interpretation of the written status of tefillin to poke fun: 'to claim that a written formula is magic makes *us* laugh' (emphasis mine). The pronoun here is indicative of the distance that Lombroso takes from his subject: he himself is part of the laughing crowd, as far from the object of derision as possible. Lombroso's feelings toward Orthodox Jews are clear in this passage, as he remarks, 'Fortunately there are few of them.' We must ask ourselves why a scientist would make such a statement if he in fact did not share the prejudices from which he claims to defend them.

The notion of magic and miracles contained within an object that Lombroso discusses here brings to mind the relic, about which his text is silent. This particular category of objects, because of their past contiguous or metonymic relation to a holy body or holy object, incorporates qualities of the divine and more specifically the capacity to perform miracles;[9]

they are not only objects of faith but represent faith itself. The powers of relics are mysterious and lie beyond the realm of reason, just as Lombroso attributes the power of tefillin to 'sad mysteries.' They emphasize the physical nature of faith, the materiality of religious belief. In his analysis, Lombroso seems to be primarily attacking the language contained in the tefillin, but in fact, it is the physicality and visibility of the object containing the writing that are the intended target, and this is reminiscent of the logic of the relic that renders it holy and worthy of faith. Lombroso's objections to Jewish practices are based largely on the *perception* of these practices, in other words, the ways in which cultural and religious difference is made visible and tangible. It is not the writing of the Torah he criticizes, or the role of this text in Judaism, but the fact that these writings are contained within a physical object that can be seen, that marks difference, and that can be ridiculed because of this.

Lombroso clearly has in mind the logic of the Christian relic in his denigration of tefillin, which are actually unlike relics in their function and meaning. It is not that he is attacking the logic of what makes a relic worthy of faith, but rather that in his view the tefillin are aberrational: they are linguistic rather than material; they are Jewish rather than Catholic. The tefillin thus appear in Lombroso's assessment as a poorly conceived embarrassment, a relic that does not know how to behave. Once again, it is what is contained in the writing in the tefillin that makes them powerful within Judaism, not that it *is* writing per se, just as it is the material relationship with a holy body that renders a relic powerful, not what it is in itself.

Elsewhere in his text, Lombroso again points out *gergo* [jargon] as another difference that marginalizes the Jew. Difference is perceived most dramatically when it is visual or aural, and language has long been a crucial site of attention in the history of antisemitism. According to the theorists of antisemitism, the use of Hebrew or Yiddish was the vilifying mark of distinction that set the Jews apart. Throughout history, and especially during the Renaissance, language was overdetermined as the most important demarcation of the radical split between Christianity and Judaism, the location of fundamental theological differences. The displacement of theology onto language translated linguistic difference into a social sign.

Gilman writes that Hebrew and then Yiddish were perceived as secret or hidden languages with magical properties that were thought to conceal from the Christian world religious and social differences that denied Christianity. The language of the Jews was thus perceived as both foreign language and discourse; as Gilman says, 'It is evident that the myth-building that surrounds the concept of a 'hidden' language of the Jews links both language and discourse in the stereotype of the Jew.'[10] Lombroso's choice of language as a point of attack thus fits into a long tradition of antisemitism: a disquisition on discourse as that which separates and distinguishes Jews and ultimately confuses their culture with the theology of Judaism. In his analysis of the internalization of self-hatred on the part of Jewish writers, Gilman concludes that 'only in those moments in their writings when they choose (or are forced) to deal with 'Jewish' topics will this sense of anxiety surface.'[11] Lombroso belongs to this category. His theories about other groups, however, betray a strong anxiety and tendency toward overdetermination and confusion when he is confronted with the question of otherness in general. This further demonstrates the interconnected nature of beliefs about people and practices marked as different.

In another chapter, Lombroso discusses the status of Jews and Judaism in relation to modernity: 'I maintain, moreover, that the majority of them are not moral, and feel more the yearning and greed for power than for good. But this, too, one explains through the practices of our epoch. Representative of modernity, they unfortunately bear its wounds.'[12] Both too atavistic and too modern, the Jews become scapegoats for the modern age. The contradiction is obvious: Lombroso has elsewhere said, repeatedly, that the Jews do not sufficiently conform in either habit, custom, or dress to the countries in which they live. How then could they bear the wounds of modernity if in fact, as he suggests, they are living in the past? The word he uses for wounds is a telling one, *piaga,* a term that may also refer to stigmata.[13] The concept of stigmata, evoking the wounds of Jesus, provides a clue to the religious and cultural subtext that informs and directs Lombroso's analysis of the Jews. He uses images and symbols from Christianity as points through which he can unfavorably compare the Jews. Later in the same chapter, he speaks of certain Jews as *mezzo-santi,* [half-saints], giving as an example a figure who he claims was viewed as a new Christ: 'Chesojub, whom Russia killed, but whom the world adored as much as a new Christ.'[14]

Lombroso thus presents the figure of the Jew as at once atavistic and modern. He reads language and religious customs as primitive, yet the Jew is made to represent the worst of modernity.[15] Finally, Lombroso employs a Christian logic and vocabulary of relics, saints, and Jesus in order to analyze and then stigmatize difference.

Lombroso's use of Christian metaphors to measure difference is clearly indexical in function. It is also revealing that he adopts the language of the scientists before him who had studied hysteria and labeled the signs of it 'stigmata.' Not only do stigmata refer to the wounds of Jesus, the verb *to stigmatize,* to label in a negative way, has further compelling shades of significance. The referent is both physical, as it refers to the wounds of Jesus left by the nails of the cross, and cultural, as it refers to that which is different and undesirable. Lombroso's term is truly ironic in this particular context: the Jewish scientist Lombroso uses stigmata to refer to the marks of difference apparent on the bodies of criminals. In *La donna delinquente,* he employs it metaphorically: 'An important stigmata of degeneration is in many female born criminals the lack of maternal affection.'[16] His own stigmatization as a Jew can thus be seen as displaced onto the even more unfortunate and stigmatized body of the criminal, the woman, and the all-so-distant figure of the Orthodox Jew he discusses in this text.

The logic of cultural difference becomes an instrument of derision as Lombroso attempts to explicate and then make absurd the practice of religious ritual. In this text, on the surface an 'impartial,' 'scientific' defense of the Jews, he adopts the logic of antisemitism in order to analyze their practices. He attacks the Jews for their cultural difference, for those activities that in fact make them Jewish, and he singles out their alleged attitudes toward language as the basis of his critique. Purportedly an examination of the relationship between antisemitism and modern science, the text quickly changes direction. It soon becomes clear that it is not really a book on this topic at all, but rather one on two related subjects: who the Jews are and how Lombroso feels about that. The text would have been more accurately entitled 'Antisemitism and the Modern Scientist' – the scientist, of course, a Jewish one, represented by Lombroso himself.

The conclusion reached at the end of his analysis is that assimilation is the answer to the problem of antisemitism – in other words, the total obliteration of difference. In the last chapter of the text, a different kind of logic is employed in Lombroso's final assessment of cultural practices as he explains the need for assimilation:

It's time for the Jews to persuade themselves that many of their rituals belong to other epochs and that their useless strangeness (matzoh, for example, or circumcision) makes one think of profane customs for which they feel the greatest repulsion. If all religions have modified their essence, not just their appearance, according to the times, why can't they at least modify appearances? Why don't they renounce that savage wounding that is circumcision, those multiple fetishes of sacred writing or of some of its sentences, which they scatter around their houses and even tie to their bodies, just like amulets, preserving without knowing it that adoration of letters that its first discoverers had and which savages still have?'[17]

49

Lombroso spells out exactly what it is that bothers him about the Jews: the dress, customs, and religious habits that separate them from other people. And he makes it equally clear that it is the *appearance* of these customs he finds the most troubling. He goes further in his assessment of tefillin and of mezuzahs, calling them 'fetishes.'[18]

The desire that Jews give up their religious practices because they are outmoded, irrational, and so forth is based on a logic of culture that becomes meaningless if applied to religion. The equivalent would be to tell Catholics to renounce the concept of the Virgin Mary because such a story is medically or scientifically impossible and is based on a primitive story that modern science has proved untenable. Seen in this light, applying what Lombroso would call scientific logic to religion plainly does not work to the benefit of either discipline. Lombroso's use of Christian metaphors to measure the difference of the Jews further signals his distance from the subject at hand and demonstrates that the logic he uses is not 'scientific' at all but rather based on the rules of a different culture.

In attempting to defend the Jews from the racist rhetoric of antisemitism, Lombroso has adopted the equally racist logic of the erasure of difference. Assimilation for the Jews in the late nineteenth century was a difficult and complicated issue. The assimilationist movement did not signal an overt attempt to leave Judaism behind and convert to Christianity; it was more often an attempt to move away from Orthodoxy. Its ramifications are, nonetheless, as serious as outright conversion. Even as popular and important a figure as Theodor Herzl, known as the father of Zionism, became an important protagonist in the debates regarding the favorability of assimilation. As Steven Beller asserts in *Vienna and the Jews, 1867–1938,* 'Herzl wanted to free the Jews from what he saw as the debilitating state of being outsiders in a hostile society, and hence make Jews normal, as it were.'[19] Both assimilation and a physical exodus to another place were seen as potential ways to eliminate the uncomfortable status of marginality;

they are two sides of the same coin. Herzl's solution was Zionism, arguing for a land where Jews would not be outsiders.[20] Lombroso's solution was instead the obliteration of difference, and he of course was hardly unique in this respect.[21] It must be remembered as well that Lombroso's liberalism no doubt played a role in his assimilationist ideas, although liberalism and its frequent anticlericalism are not sufficient in themselves to explain his theories regarding Jews.[22]

Lombroso's defense of the Jews lies almost entirely in his criticism of the sense of proportion involved in antisemitism. To his credit, he does take on the most ferocious theorists of antisemitism, destroying their arguments in his discussion of the problem. He does not believe that cultural differences, although they encourage divisiveness and derision, justify the viciousness of antisemitism, and he describes extreme antisemitism as a disease in itself. He discusses the political scope of antisemitism and how it has been used by political factions for their own ends. 'Another epidemic bacillus' is the term he uses at one point to describe that which propagates antisemitism, and elsewhere he calls these factors 'the germs of the illness.'[23] Lombroso is using terms he can understand within a scientific framework of illness – an illness that, by implication, has a potential cure. To continue this metaphor, however, one must conclude that his cure for the illness is the demise of the patient – no more germs, so no more epidemic.

To conclude this analysis of Lombroso's writings on Judaism, it is useful to look at another of his texts. Stigmata, or physical marks of difference and exclusion (for that is really what the stigmata represent), are present in Lombroso's thoughts on Jews in this second text in a somewhat different form. In the introduction to *Genio e degenerazione: nuovi studi e nuove battaglie* [Genius and Degeneration: New Studies and New Battles], written late in his career, Lombroso situates the question of the relationship of evolution and the Jews in the following way:

But the natural sciences demonstrate to us that evolution is never complete, and that a great evolution in one direction is always accompanied by an arrest in other directions. We see, in fact, peoples remarkably advanced in one area present extraordinary regressions in others. Thus the Jews who had gone with Christ up until communism, with Moses until monotheism, with Marx until socialism, who created the IOU, formed the nucleus of bourgeois capitalism (even though now they are goading the fourth state against this). One finds them to be part of all the most advanced evolutions, yet they not only lose the personal courage and the patriotic energy that had caused even the Roman to marvel at the spectacle of an entire city commit suicide rather than surrender, but still adopt religiously the *quippu* (alphabet knots) on their prayer shawls, and stone weapons for circumcision, and preserve in this custom a leftover from cannibalism. In politics, then, they always show an excess of conservatism. As soon as they settle for a while in a country, they preserve its customs, even clothes when these have already disappeared in the country of origin; sometimes even the language.[24]

This argument presents another summary of Lombroso's critique of the Jews and, moreover, contains a stronger reaction to the issue of circumcision. He claims in this text that circumcision was performed with stone weapons. In *L'antisemitismo e le scienze moderne,* he had written that it was accomplished with the teeth: 'He even reaches the point of using his teeth as well as stone knives for the cruel practice of circumcision, as did our cave ancestors.'[25] But here Lombroso has added the charge of cannibalism as he asserts that circumcision shows leftover traces of this practice.

Lombroso's method of analysis in this text is far removed from the claims made in the preface. He makes it clear that he has consulted both sides, as it were: Jewish writers for their concepts of what Jewish culture and religion are all about and the racist theorists for their reasoning. He treats both with guarded respect, since his goal is after all impartiality. As we have seen, in the text on women Lombroso challenged the lack of opportunity for women and their exploitation by men. His divided opinion arose largely from his own contradictory views, since the only theorist on the exploitation of women he cited was himself. In this text on antisemitism, Lombroso also tries to present more than one point of view. Rather than an understanding of what society must be like for women, which seems to be his motivation for some of the remarks he makes in the preface regarding opportunity, here he limits his comprehension of what it could be like to be Jewish to coldly citing some Jewish writers, without any real sympathy – or even empathy – for the Jews themselves. The distance that he imposes on his subject is much greater than we have seen in *La donna delinquente.*

As an anthropological approach, Lombroso's method of analysis clearly lacks impartiality or sophistication; as an approach whose scientific method is borrowed from psychiatry, it reveals perhaps more the unmediated psychological reactions of the writer himself. The most crucial point of contention Lombroso seems most interested in is circumcision. It is mentioned at least six or seven times in this text and appears in other texts, returned to obsessively as a term of analysis that shifts as he variously explains the origin of the rite as savage, atavistic, primitive, and a return to cannibalism and even to human sacrifice.

Teeth, cannibalism, circumcision – we can leave aside for the moment the understanding that Lombroso himself was most probably circumcised. It was necessary for every Jewish male, and Lombroso's family was, after all, Jewish. Further, there would seem to be little doubt that he also resented it tremendously. Why is it that Lombroso makes these dark connections between tearing skin with the teeth, stone weapons, and cannibalism? Is this once again a charge of atavism and nothing more? Examining another text may provide part of an answer. Lombroso and his theories appear as protagonists in Bram Stoker's *Dracula,* as Count Dracula is compared to a

Lombrosian criminal: 'The Count is a criminal and of criminal type. Nordau and Lombroso would so classify him, and qua criminal he is of imperfectly formed mind.'[26] Even more interesting is the description of Dracula at the beginning of the novel, when Jonathan Harker sees him for the first time. A comparison of Harker's depiction with Lombroso's descriptions of born criminals has been made by Leonard Wolf:

> Harker: 'His [the Count's] face was . . . aquiline, with high bridge of the thin nose and peculiarly arched nostrils . . .'
> Lombroso: '[The criminal's] nose on the contrary . . . is often aquiline like the beak of a bird of prey.'
> Harker: 'His eyebrows were very massive, almost meeting over the nose . . .'
> Lombroso: 'The eyebrows are bushy and tend to meet across the nose.'
> Harker: '. . . his ears were pale and at the tops extremely pointed'
> Lombroso: 'with a protuberance on the upper part of the posterior margin . . . a relic of the pointed ear . . .'[27]

The first and most obvious point here is that Stoker had come into contact with Lombroso's theories – not surprising, given the widespread nature of their influence – and used this description in his text, first published in 1897. What is more interesting, though, is the connection made by Lombroso between cannibalism and circumcision performed with the teeth in the light of how the stereotype of the Lombrosian criminal was read by the public and assimilated into popular culture. Sander Gilman, in his intriguing article on Jack the Ripper, analyzes the police portrait of the unknown killer nicknamed 'Jack.' He compares it not only to the Lombrosian description of a sadistic criminal but also to the stereotype of the Eastern European Jew: 'What is striking is that the image of 'Jack' is also set. He is the caricature of the Eastern Jew. Indeed, the official description of 'Jack' was that of a man "aged 37, rather dark beard and moustache, dark jacket and trousers, black felt hat, spoke with a foreign accent." '[28] Gilman recounts that some of the antisemitic graffiti that began to appear made direct references to Jack's being Jewish and tells us that the playwright Frank Wedekind incorporates Jack as a character in one of his plays, 'Pandora's Box,' and describes him in terms very similar to the Lombrosian sadist.

What surfaces is a cultural theme of blood, vampirism, cannibalism, and sexual perversion all linked to the antisemitism prevalent at the time. What is particularly compelling is the role that Lombroso plays in the establishment of this theme. He appears in two manifestations: his direct pronouncements on circumcision, linking it to cannibalism and teeth, and his descriptions of criminals – which are strikingly close to some of the stereotypes of Eastern European Jews. It is no accident that Stoker would have picked up Lombroso's description of the criminal and used it to portray a vampire.[29] Lombroso's notions of what is criminal, what is female, and finally what is Jewish ultimately belong to an entirely cultural realm of imagined monsters. These categories and the way in which they are problematized reveal what was considered monstrous in late nineteenth-century culture. They demonstrate as well a social fantasy about the nature of difference.

Lombroso, Women, and Jews

As we have seen from the preceding chapter, Lombroso draws heavily on preexisting ideas about women, both from recapitulationist theory and from other theories of gender difference that were popular at the time. His most obvious 'contribution' to an understanding of the nature of woman, his linking of the criminal and the prostitute to woman's identity in a programmatic categorization, was also the most controversial part of his theory on women, as his contemporary Havelock Ellis notes, in his preface to *The Criminal,* by calling the work 'deeply interesting though often debatable.'[30] The controversial nature of Lombroso's ideas on women is paralleled by his theories concerning the Jews. His conclusions regarding the two begin to resemble one another, because his theories about them are quite similar.[31]

The goal of *L'antisemitismo e le scienze moderne* is like that of Lombroso and Ferrero's text on women: an attempt to understand the marginalized group, why they are in such a position in culture, and how it is they deserve their status. The most notable difference between the two texts is the methods of analysis used and the way in which Lombroso engages his sources. As I have already mentioned, in *La donna delinquente,* Lombroso and Ferrero make copious references to other thinkers on the subject of women. So frequent and undifferentiated are these references and quotations that at times the text reads like a compendium of opinions regarding women that has no clear authorship at all. The text on Jews, however, uses fewer references and engages active debate with them, rather than merely parroting the references to back up the authors' own views.

There is a long moment in *La donna delinquente* when the subjects of women and Jews intersect. This most troubling passage in Lombroso's evaluation of what is Jewish seems to come about by accident, when he is occupied in assessing the 'real' nature of woman. At a certain point in *La donna delinquente,* Lombroso provides a short history of prostitution divided into sections, one of which deals with 'sacred prostitution' within religious sects. It is here that Lombroso's prejudicial opinions regarding Jews and women are most clear – namely, when the two categories collide and the topic becomes Jewish women, or, more specifically, Jewish prostitutes. At the beginning of the section, Lombroso makes the following statement:

> Among the Jews, before the definitive version of the Tablets of Law, the father had the right to sell the daughter to a man who would make of her his concubine for a period of time established by the sales contract. The daughter sold in this way for the profit of her father did not gain anything from the forced relinquishing of her body, except in the case where

the man would engage her to his son and so would substitute her with another concubine. The Jews thus trafficked in the prostitution of their own daughters.[32]

This passage brings up several crucial questions of interpretation. Could this terrible accusation leveled by Lombroso possibly have been true in some way? Could Lombroso have had a source for this statement, even a spurious one? The answer to the first question is probably no, and to the second, possibly yes.[33] But the kinds of questions generated by this passage go well beyond any localized ones in the sense of looking at Biblical history and its interpreters through the centuries in order to determine whether Lombroso was following a historical source. More suggestive is the fact that he gives the episode as much emphasis as he does and that he frames certain questions within the context of these passages. Other forms of 'religious prostitution' merit a paragraph here, a sentence there, in this chapter, but there are three full pages devoted to this discussion of the role of the Jews in prostitution and other references elsewhere in the text. Reading the book, one gets the impression that Lombroso makes the connection between Jews and prostitutes just as often as he can.

This collision – or collusion – of the figure of the Jew and that of woman creates a great moment of tension in the text. An interpretation of the passage and the images embedded within it makes clear how strong this tension is and precisely what is at stake for Lombroso in the relationship between Jew and woman. The first image is the stereotype of the greedy Jew who capitalizes on the body of his female child, emphasized with the words 'for the profit of her father' in the second line of the passage. Even more insidious is the notion that somehow she is being deprived of the profit she herself could have made. Lombroso is careful to point this out, as he says, 'the daughter sold in this way did not gain anything' – as if her profit from prostitution would have made this practice acceptable. The second image is that of the Jewish woman as prostitute. Here the daughter is figured as a potential one who is stymied by her father's insistence on making the profit himself. This last point is emphasized once again by the statement at the end of the passage: 'The Jews trafficked thus in the prostitution of their own daughters.' The connection of Jews to prostitutes made in early modern culture has been analyzed by Gilman in his article 'I'm Down on Whores': Race and Gender in Victorian London,' in which he says, 'The relationship between the Jew and the prostitute also has a social dimension. For both Jew and prostitute have but one interest, the conversion of sex into money or money into sex.'[34] This is an apt description of Lombroso's passage, as the two parties, father and daughter, are literally *competing* for the right to profit from her body.

The intensity of this intersection of women and Jews derails outright the scientific methodology employed in this work. This point is even more noticeable in a text that obsessively cites its sources, whether they be measurements from studies or proverbs, but here does not cite other scholars at all. There is a self-confidence about the material presented in the section that creates a different tone than we find elsewhere in Lombroso's work. Usually in his texts there seems to be the assumption that citations from other experts, numbers from studies, measurements, and so on are *required,* necessary, in some way, to back up what he is saying, even if these 'proofs' are potentially specious, as I have shown above. In this section there is the sense that, because he is dealing with a Biblical text, in other words, common cultural knowledge – and perhaps *also* because he is Jewish and it is his forebears whose behavior he is analyzing – he does not need to cite anyone else and is free to come up with these imaginative and pejorative interpretations.

Already in this text we have seen a mingling of terms between the 'normal' woman, the prostitute, and the criminal. When the figure of the Jewish father is introduced as another player in Lombroso's drama of cultural difference, the confusion becomes so great that the potential for the kind of overt fictionalization we see in the passage above is created.

In this section, Lombroso also discusses the attempts made by Moses to reform the Jews' prostitution practices and to discourage them from following the cults of Baal and Moloch:

> Among the Jews, however, before the reforms of Moses, sacred prostitution was widely diffused; in fact the legislative work of Moses was above all a fight against the phallic cults of Moloch and Baal-Fegor, common to the semitic populations. Moses tried to wipe out religious prostitution, but he didn't succeed, because traces of religious prostitution are found in holy books up until the period of the Maccabees. . . . Such were the excesses of the Israelites with the Moabite women who are connected to a phallic cult. These women had raised tents and opened shops from Bet-Aiscimot to Ar-Ascaleg: there they sold every kind of jewelry, and the Jews ate and drank in the middle of this camp of prostitution (Numbers 25). The prophet Ezekiel has left us with a frightening portrait of Jewish corruption; one reads only of courtesans dressed in silks and embroidery, gleaming with jewels and covered with perfumes, and infamous scenes of fornication everywhere. The temple of Jerusalem at the time of the Maccabees, one and a half centuries before Jesus Christ, was still the commercial arena of the prostitutes who came there looking to practice their profession.[35]

There seems to be a deliberate mixing up of Jews, Canaanites, and biblical Israelites in this passage that furthers the confusions regarding who is following which prostitution cult and, more important (and most likely Lombroso's point here), implicates the biblical Jews in diverse kinds of sexual misconduct.[36] At best, we can view this as a confusion of different biblical laws regarding the legislation of slaves and marriage contracts. At worst, it is a deliberate misreading and misinterpretation of the story of the biblical Jews, designed to link them to cults of prostitution and to infer a connection between pernicious antisemitic caricatures and biblical paradigms, as if the stereotypical Jew-as-profiteer were already prominent among these first biblical Jews and thus is an inseparable part of Jewishness. The identity of these biblical Jews would seem to furnish a key for Lombroso's understanding of the meaning of contemporary Judaism. It is also noteworthy that he uses the term *Gesù Cristo* to refer to Jesus. The title 'Christ,' savior, implies belief in the tenets of Christianity and is not typically used by Jews.

Another passage in the section on adultery describes a well-known biblical paragraph treating suspected adultery and how Moses dealt with the issue:

> In order to reassure husbands who suspected of adultery their wives who were sick with gonorrhea, Moses ordered that, when the wife accused the husband of giving her the disease, both would go before the priest. The husband offered to his wife a bread made of barley without oil, called the bread of jealousy; the priest put the bread in the hands of the woman and held in his own the bitter waters that contained the curse: 'If no man has slept with you,' said the priest, 'and if in being submissive to your husband you have not been sullied, then let these waters not affect you. But if the contrary has occurred, if you have been impure and fornicated with others, let the Eternal abandon you to the execration to which you have sworn yourself, and let these cursed waters enter your viscera and make your belly swell and your thigh dry up.' The woman answered amen and drank the bitter waters. If later the woman's belly swelled and her thigh dried up, she was convicted of adultery and became infamous in the eyes of Israel. The husband, on the contrary, whom everyone pitied like an innocent victim, found himself vindicated, if not healed.[37]

Lombroso gets this episode almost right, but a significant addition changes the tone of the passage. Numbers 5 is the biblical source for this story, and it seems that this practice of determining the guilt or innocence of the wife regarding the accusation of adultery did exist. The potion she was made to drink was not in itself a harmful one, since it was made from a little dust from the floor of the temple and water. Perhaps the efficacy of this method depended entirely on the psychology of guilt rather than on a physiological reaction to the potion. But the connection of adultery and gonorrhea is *not* part of this biblical episode. The connection between disease – more specifically, sexual disease – and Jewish life and sexuality, however, is made by Lombroso. The end of the passage shows a guileful move on the part of the author when it comes to the ultimate position in which he places the husband. He is exculpated and pitied as an innocent victim if his wife shows signs of guilt – but he is *not* cured of the disease. In what seems to be an inevitable fate, he too is polluted by the sexual sins of the Jewish woman.

Lombroso's portrait of woman in *La donna delinquente* strongly resembles that of the Orthodox Jew. Woman, as prostitute, is criticized for exhibiting her difference through virility; at the same time she is scorned for attempting to hide this difference through makeup and dress. The modern-day prostitute is an atavistic phenomenon. The Orthodox Jew is likewise criticized for displaying his difference through dress and is also described as a throwback. His figure stands to the Jew as the prostitute is linked to woman: the most atavistic representation. The sexual connection that Lombroso has conferred in these passages further joins the prostitute and the Orthodox Jew in presenting the figure of the atavistic Jewish woman: part prostitute and sexually defamed.

Lombroso's rewritings of biblical episodes include not only charges of sexual misconduct but also the accusation of disease. His implicit definition of the Jew in these passages brings us to the question of the self-identity of the author. What is at stake for an author like Lombroso, Jewish himself but first and foremost a scientist, when he confronts the issues of the identity of the Jews, both modern and biblical? The next chapter will address questions of Lombroso's Jewish self-identity while looking at the cases of Otto Weininger and Franz Boas as points of comparison.

CHAPTER FOUR

PORTRAITS OF SELF-ABNEGATION

I n the previous chapter, we saw how Lombroso rewrote biblical episodes to present his own view of Jewish sexuality, particularly that of Jewish women. Certain pejorative images of Jews and women are not only woven into his analysis, they also furnish the basis of his argument and demonstrate how prejudice can affect both the methodology with which he operates and the conclusions that he draws. The kinds of bias apparent in Lombroso's thought raises the crucial question of his own self-identity. Robert Oden, in his 'Religious Identity and the Sacred Prostitution Accusation,' queries the identity of the accuser as he investigates the nature of accusations of sacred prostitution:

> Perhaps sacred prostitution ought to be investigated as an accusation rather than as a reality. Perhaps, then, this alleged practice belongs in the same category with cannibalism, sodomy, and abhorrent dietary and sexual practices generally – that is to say, in the category of charges that one society levels against others as part of that society's process of self-definition. . . . Viewed in this way, the accusation that other societies utilize religious personnel as part of sacred sexual rites surely tells us something about those who formulate and repeat the accusation. . . . [T]he accusation may tell us little or nothing about those religions against which the charge is leveled.[1]

The accusatory nature of Lombroso's agenda regarding Jewish women is better understood in the light of Oden's theory concerning the identity of the accuser in relation to the accusations made. The issue of his Jewish identity raised by a reading of his views brings us to some more general questions regarding Jews who attack Jews and Judaism, and 'self-hatred,' the term most commonly used to describe such Jews.

The history of the usage of the term begins in 1930 with Theodore Lessing's *Der jüdische Selbtshass* [Jewish Self-Hatred], at the culmination of a crucial period for European Jewry. The late nineteenth century and the beginning of the twentieth century saw a number of heated debates regarding Jews come to light from both inside and outside the Jewish community. It was at once a period of great antisemitism in Germany and Austria and a time of great self-affirmation for Jews, as figures like Theodor Herzl and Max Nordau envisioned the state of Israel and its implications for the Jews. A theme of Jewish self-abnegation also became common as Jews tried to negotiate new freedoms at the end of the era of the ghettos, a period that included rising antisemitism. The dialectical relationship of certain Jewish individuals with their identity became an issue, as the words 'not Jewish' were seen as an ever-elusive and ultimately unattainable goal. For some Jews, the attainment of this goal would have signaled the end of prejudice against them.

There is a limited bibliography on Jewish self-hatred extending from Lessing to contemporary thinkers trying to come to grips with a difficult issue.[2] The issue of converted Jews whose internalized hatred spurs them to write antisemitic tracts is a central topic in Sander Gilman's *Jewish Self-Hatred: Antisemitism and the Hidden Language of the Jews.* The writers Gilman describes have for the most part taken on the role of the fanatic who urges conversion and/or that of the informer who relates the 'true nature' and faults of the Jews to the Christian world.

Paul Marcus and Alan Rosenberg have also written on self-hatred, pointing out that the label is often used as a political weapon when there is disagreement, for example, 'One spokesman for a particular Jewish group labels as a self-hater another Jewish leader who disagrees with his position.' This charge has been levied in cases ranging wildly from Karl Marx to Otto Weininger to a Jew who merely intermarries. Marcus and Rosenberg maintain that the label is not only provocative but is also ill defined and 'generates much heat but no light.' The question of definition raised by the authors shows why 'self-hatred' is so vague and is used in a such a variety of circumstances. They point out that neither the term 'Jewish' nor 'self' is defined by the user: 'The term "Jewish" is also very difficult to define clearly. What is apparent from the literature, however, is that when authors write about JSH [Jewish self-hatred], they imply that they have an implicit notion of what constitutes Jewishness. This notion is usually not spelled out by the writer. It is well known that the question of who is a Jew and what constitutes authentic Jewishness is an exceedingly complex issue, and that there is no consensus even about basic matters.'[3]

The lack of clarity regarding the term 'Jewish' in particular is pertinent to an understanding of how Lombroso's place vis-à-vis the category of 'self-hating Jews.' What could Jewish self-hatred be for Lombroso? It is impossible to answer this question unless we understand first what he himself understood as Jewish. Our primary clue here is the way he implicitly defines Jewishness in his writings. Jewishness for Lombroso constitutes the sum of the visibility of its representatives, in other words, who looks and 'acts' Jewish and how that is perceived by the non-Jewish community, as I have outlined in chapter 3 above. It is important to keep in mind that he attacks the visibility of Jewish cultural and religious practices, in other words, that he does not attack Judaism, in other words theology, but only practice. What is missing in his critique is a reckoning of what Jewishness is *besides* visible difference from the rest of the community. As it is, his account of Jewishness lacks an account of Judaism and is thus by default a highly prejudicial enterprise. So does this make Lombroso a self-hating Jew? Marcus and Rosenberg discuss other factors that should be taken into account before this label is applied, including complicity with antisemitic policies on the part of individuals or the government, acts of antisemitism, and so on. Religious affiliation and degree of assimilation are not enough in themselves to determine whether or not an individual is self-hating, according to the authors, which seems reasonable enough. It does not appear from the historical data available that Lombroso engaged in acts of antisemitism, nor was he alive in an age that would have required an act of identification on his part. All we have to go on are his texts that discuss Jews from an anthropological point of view.

A case in some ways similar to Lombroso's, that of cultural anthropologist Franz Boas, may shed more light on how to place Lombroso within the tradition of Jewish authors who denigrate their own origins. Boas, who developed what is now accepted as the modern definition of culture, formulated theories that were generally antiassimilationist, except when it came to the Jews. He left Germany and came to the United States in 1884, becoming a permanent resident in 1888. During his life in the United States, Boas affirmed his identity as a German-American but 'advocated assimilation to the point of literal disappearance for Jews.'[4] Leonard Glick argues that when it came to other ethnic groups 'with which he has not personally identified – Blacks and American Indians – he seems to have adopted a somewhat intermediate position: he anticipated their ultimate assimilation but recognized and supported their need for a sense of pride in their own heritage.'[5]

In 1921, Boas said about the problem of prejudice, 'Thus it would seem that man being what he is, the Negro problem will not disappear in America until the Negro blood has been so much diluted that it will no longer be recognized just as anti-Semitism will not disappear until the last vestiges of the Jew as a Jew has disappeared.'[6] Boas also later made the following observations about his own upbringing as a Jew and his views on tradition:

My parents had broken through the shackles of dogma. My father had retained an emotional affection for the ceremonial of his parental home without allowing it to influence his intellectual freedom. Thus I was spared the struggle against religious dogma that besets the lives of so many young people. . . . The psychological origin of the implicit belief in the authority of tradition, which was so foreign to my mind and which had shocked me at an earlier time, became a problem that engaged my thought for many years. In fact, my whole outlook upon social life is determined by the question: how can we recognize the shackles that tradition has laid upon us? For when we recognize them, we are also able to break them.[7]

The first citation from Boas's work demonstrates a connection between the onerous reality of prejudice and a desire for assimilation as a way to escape it. His later remarks concerning the grip of tradition and the relationship of his own family to it demonstrate Boas's attitudes toward his identity as a Jew, the difficulty he clearly felt in breaking away entirely, and his notion that an understanding of how the 'shackles' of tradition work can lead to their rending. What these remarks share is a strategy, namely, that of assimilation, either as a solution for prejudice or as a means to escape stifling tradition.

So why is it that Boas changes his attitudes about the pride in heritage he advocates for others when it comes to the Jews? It would seem once again to be a question of personal identification and the problems this causes for the scholar himself. Glick maintains that Boas was in many ways a typical product of his generation: he was brought up in a Germany that was experiencing a virulent wave of antisemitism and was physically attacked at the university by other students because he was a Jew. Along with many other German Jews, he had given up the struggle to assimilate into a hostile German culture.[8] In Boas's case, like that of Lombroso, there is a contradiction between the way he theorizes about other groups and his relation to his own; he is blinded by his own identification with the group he is studying. Total assimilation presents itself as a way of eliminating that uncomfortable position. The major differences between Lombroso's and Boas's motivations for their positions on Jews rest on the fact that Boas was brought up in a society overtly hostile to Jews, while Lombroso was not. Boas confines his hostility toward Judaism to remarks regarding the desirability of assimilation; Lombroso is the author of outright attacks on the Jews in addition to projecting assimilation as the solution to antisemitism.

Would the label of self-hatred then fit Franz Boas? It is probably too severe for the kind of self-abnegation, embarrassment, and blindness apparent in his attitudes toward Jews. Should the urge to abandon one's own kind because the going gets too rough always be labeled self-hatred? Could his actions not equally be defined as self-preservation in an age of severe discrimination? An important distinction that must be drawn between figures like Boas and Lombroso is that Boas did not openly attack the Jews. Lombroso did, and therefore belongs in a different category. Both, however, used the authority of science to justify their opinions and feelings about Jews: Boas as a cultural anthropologist, Lombroso as a criminal anthropologist.

Some reflection regarding the differences between the terms 'Jewish antisemitism' and 'Jewish self-hatred' will help us further understand the distinctions between Lombroso and Boas. 'Jewish self-hatred' points to a pathology on the part of the self-hater, internalized prejudice. Rather than hate those others who represent the qualities he believes to be negative, he turns his disgust on himself. Self-hatred also has more widespread implications: in other words, self-hatred does not in fact stop with the self but is extended to other members of the group in question. Jewish antisemitism, to the contrary, points to the product of the disease rather than the disease itself: the prejudices against Jews developed by the Jew, and ostensibly acted on in some way, whether through prejudicial acts or writings. The first formulation, Jewish self-hatred, does not escape the discourse of blaming the victim. Like the racism implicit in the category of 'race,' it is inextricably bound up with that which it seeks to escape.[9] This is not to say that the need for such a term does not exist (because in some cases, such as that of Otto Weininger, the indication of a pathology is appropriate) but rather to point out the problems in its usage. Instead, another term is needed to point out ambivalence and prejudice that is not as pernicious as what is implied in either Jewish self-hatred or Jewish antisemitism. Two terms that suggest themselves are *self-denial*, the refusal of the figure in question to understand or acknowledge his or her own identification with Jews, and *self-abnegation*, the partial erasure of identity that results from this refusal or inability. Neither term is fully sufficient to explain what is essentially a very complicated phenomenon that differs in its intensity and expression from case to case. They do, however, at least partially escape the pathology of the label of self-hatred and the severity of that of antisemitism. They distinguish varying degrees of extremity and are appropriate in the cases of both Lombroso and Boas.

An examination of a third figure, Otto Weininger, who appeared on the intellectual scene a generation after Lombroso, will make the distinctions between self-hatred, self-denial, and self-abnegation even clearer. Weininger, a young Austrian Jew who converted to Protestantism, wrote a text entitled *Sex and Character,* published in 1903. His short life (he committed suicide at the age of twenty-three in the room where Beethoven died) and rather dramatic career would be nonetheless relatively unremarkable were it not for the tremendous influence his theories had on the next generation of thinkers. Writers as diverse as Elias Canetti, James Joyce, and Italo Svevo read and embraced his theories in varying degrees and interpreted them in their works.[10]

Weininger's treatment of Jews and women is more complicated than a simple diatribe against the two groups. In his insistence that he is talking about 'qualities' or 'tendencies' rather than 'people,' Weininger intrigued his intellectual generation by his formulation of women and Jews into a recognizable group of traits that are, however, mostly disembodied. His description of what Judaism and antisemitism are provides a kind of road map for self-hatred: 'I must however, make clear what I mean by Judaism; I mean neither a race nor a people nor a recognised creed. I think of it as a tendency of the mind, as a psychological constitution which is a possibility for all mankind, but which has become actual in the most conspicuous fashion only amongst the Jews. Antisemitism itself will confirm my point of view.'[11]

This argument is a circular one on the part of Weininger, and it sets the stage for his description of antisemitism. If Judaism is a tendency of the mind and Jews are the only ones who have this tendency in a conspicuous fashion, then Jews are the only ones who are Jews, according to Weiningerian logic. We also have the 'near-Jews,' the only ones who are capable of hating the Jews:

> The purest Aryans by descent and disposition are seldom Antisemites, although they are often unpleasantly moved by some of the peculiar Jewish traits; they cannot in the least understand the Antisemite movement. . . . [T]he aggressive Antisemites, on the other hand, nearly always display certain Jewish characters, sometimes apparent in their faces, although they may have no real admixture of Jewish blood. The explanation is simple. People love in others the qualities they would like to have but do not actually have in any great degree; so also we hate in others only what we do not wish to be, and what notwithstanding we are partly.[12]

The connection to Weininger's own life is unmistakable as Weininger the convert speaks about the dynamics of self-hatred as he sees them. The incompleteness of his own conversion is made clear in his articulation of what is and what is not Jewish. Simultaneously a racial issue (as he discusses physical traits of Jews elsewhere in the chapter) and a psychological issue (as he defines Judaism as 'tendencies'), conversion is an impossibility according to the paradox set up by Weininger. Judaism both is and is not racial and is and is not a set of 'tendencies' synonymous with 'being' Jewish. And antisemites (like Weininger) find themselves trapped within the same paradox. If they hate Jews, they must be to some degree Jewish in their psychic makeup; furthermore, if they are self-hating Jews, there is absolutely no escape from this condition, whatever their new religious status. As Jeffrey Mehlman remarks, 'As Otto Weininger, the patron saint of Jewish self-hatred, already put it, the Jew characteristically hates himself *in the other*, and the Jewish *other* of the would-be assimilated Jew is the Yiddish-speaking Schlemihl.'[13]

Weininger's suicide after the publication of *Sex and Character* can be read as an inner implosion of his own contradictions regarding the identity of the Jewish other and his relationship to self-identity. Allan Janik maintains that since there is little biographical material regarding Weininger that could shed more light on his motivations, a psychological interpretation of this sort is a highly risky proposal.[14] It seems clear nonetheless that there is most likely some connection between Weininger's conversion, his writings about Jews, and his suicide. In his case, the pathology involved in his elaboration of self-hatred is clear. The connections between what he views as Jewish and the identity of those 'capable' of hating Jews dissolve into the same person: the Jew himself.

Weininger sets up distinct categories of Jew and woman and then intertwines them. Like the Jew, 'woman' does not always refer to a human being but often to the quality of the female element, the 'abstract idea,' as he calls it. In order to make direct comparisons between Judaism and woman, Weininger labels the Jew as womanly: 'Some reflection will lead to the surprising result that Judaism is saturated with femininity, with precisely those qualities the essence of which I have shown to be in the strongest opposition to the male nature.'[15] Weininger takes us through his comparison: they both lack a 'real sense of landed property,' they are 'wanting in personality,' which means they cannot grasp the 'conception of a State,' they lack dignity, they are both 'non-moral,' and they are more involved in 'sexual matters' than are Aryan men.[16]

At the end of his chapter on Judaism, Weininger lines up the opposing camps in 'our age,' as he calls it: Jewish and Christian, business and culture, female and male, race and individual. He states emphatically that there are only two poles, no middle ground, and that one must decide between the two. Here there is a clear departure from his stated intent of examining qualities, abstract ideas of Jewishness and woman, as he is now addressing real groups in what is a political as well as cultural agenda. In his final chapter he proposes that the only solution to the problem of woman is that woman should overcome her femaleness through an abandonment of sexuality. Weininger views undesirable sexuality or religion as a state to be conquered. His 'solution' calls for, quite simply, the end of the human race. It is not only the erasure of cultural, sexual, or religious difference that is advocated here.

It was in part the convolution of categories in Lombroso's work that gave a future generation of Italian intellectuals such easy access to Otto Weininger's contradictory and mingled categories of difference. The subjective reading of Judaism through the logic of Christianity is not the only moment in Lombroso in which categories are mixed. There is a confusion between male and female as well – the 'degendering' of the prostitute, the links made between female criminals and normal women, and so on – an intertwining that was echoed in a strangely familiar way ten years later in Weininger's sexual and religious 'character' study.[17]

In his meditations on women, Lombroso's misogynistic model for interpreting female behavior reinforces negative stereotypes and posits the female criminal as one who exemplifies the worst traits but who is typical of 'normal' women in many ways. Fear of what is female is categorically structured in his text as we learn that the average woman is but a criminal waiting to strike and a prostitute waiting to be unleashed. Here and elsewhere Lombroso marginalizes criminality through his measuring and categorizing the correlations between physical difference and behavior. In *La donna delinquente,* he finds himself concluding, as we have already seen, that the female criminal quite often demonstrates male characteristics. Lombroso thus blurs the distinctions between men and women both in his discussion of the criminal and in his discussions of women.

As Barbara Spackman notes in her work on Lombroso, 'In his studies of genius, of criminals and anarchists, Lombroso employs a sort of magnified metalepsis whereby groups that have appeared most recently (decadent artists, political activists, urban criminals) are described as atavistic and archaic rather than, as in Marxist discourse, the products of modern industrialization.'[18] The metalepsis that Spackman describes here is applicable as well to Lombroso's theories regarding Jews. Just as Lombroso befuddles and blurs sexual difference, he treats the Jews as at once too primitive and too modern. Another kind of distinction is challenged as well in Lombroso's mixing up cultural categories in his criticism of Jewish religious practice. Lombroso thus sets the stage for Weininger's reception in two ways: first through the widespread influence of his theories and method insofar as they promoted misogyny and antisemitism and second through a tendency toward the blurring of distinctions that is likewise seen in Weininger work. The emphasis on the physical quantification of difference present in Lombroso's theories underscored the acceptability of biologically based theories of the inferiority of certain groups popular at the time, even while he denied any validity to such theories, as he maintained that the Jews were not a single race.

These two theorists of difference, Lombroso and Weininger, share some distinct attributes. A tendency to blur the very differences that they seek to stigmatize marks a theoretical similarity between them. Just as striking is a dissimilarity in the reception of certain of their texts: Lombroso was a world-renowned criminologist, yet there is very little in print about his text on antisemitism, while Weininger, a young student of philosophy and characterology, was hailed by many important figures of his day as a genius who understood both the nature of sexual difference and the nature of the Jews.

Weininger and Lombroso differ also in that, although Weininger converted to Christianity, Lombroso never did. Gilman's portrait of the antisemitic Jew who converts and then writes against the Jews could well be a description of Weininger, and in fact he appears as a protagonist in Gilman's text. Weininger, however, further complicates the issue of Jewish antisemitism by his misogynist theories and by his insistence on making direct comparisons between women and Jews.[19] Lombroso, on the other hand, does not easily fit the portrait of the antisemitic Jew: his background shows no sign of restlessness, no conversion, and no abandonment of the faith. However, his theories about difference in women, criminals, and Jews contributed to an intellectual atmosphere in Italy that at the turn of the century was receptive to Weininger and hostile to Freud.[20]

Lombroso's reading of the motives for antisemitism and the place of the Jews in culture provides a link to Weiningerian theories of cultural and sexual difference and ways in which those theories are interpreted. Lombroso's particular brand of intolerance and the connections it had to Weininger reception in Italy are part of the cultural background that informed the web of political and social distortions of the Holocaust. Lombroso is the figure of the dispassionate scientist who banks on the impartiality of scientific method, who flinches in the face of difference, particularly his own: and then pulls out the measuring devices to show positively that difference does exist physically, even to the naked eye. According to Lombroso's theories, religious rituals and practices do not stand up to the scrutiny of positivism, although he confined his attacks on the 'ridiculousness' of religious practice to Judaism. Both Weininger and Lombroso seem to deny Judaism a theological

74

content, as they focus instead on practices as if these were disassociated from theology.

There is an even more direct link between Lombroso and Weininger: several of the footnotes in the original German edition of *Sex and Character* contain references to Lombroso, whom Weininger obviously admired and took very seriously, particularly when it came to the theories about women. Janik, in his *How Not to Interpret a Culture: Essays on the Problem of Method in the* Geisteswissenshaften, demonstrates the influence that Lombroso had on Weininger:

> Even a cursory glance at Weininger's notes and references indicates that he was heavily indebted for his data about women to a work called *La Donna Delinquente e La Prostituta* [sic] by Cesare Lombroso, Professor of Forensic Medicine and father of modern criminology. . . . Not a little of the 'empirical data' upon which Weininger based his reasoning is to be found in Lombroso's study of the female offender. For example two ideas which were to recur as central themes in *Geschlecht und Charakter,* namely that women are generally less sensitive to perceptual stimuli and the notion that women are more prone to lying than men (for which he advances eight causes) are already central themes in Lombroso's work. In fact most of the things that we find obnoxious and repugnant in *Geschlecht und Charakter* today, can be found in *La Donna Delinquente.*[21]

In the context of Weininger studies, Lombroso thus becomes doubly famous as father of criminology as well as intellectual father to Otto Weininger! The history of Weininger criticism is fraught with disagreements on how literally *Sex and Character* can or should be read and contextualized. Janik, for example, maintains the following points in carefully situating Weininger's writing: 'Firstly, I want to insist that it must be evaluated by reference to the state of biological sciences, psychology and humanistic social reform circa 1903. Secondly, I want to assert that a close reading of the text reveals a strong dialectical element in Weininger's thinking which actually renders his conclusion that the argument turns against men less paradoxical than it appears at first glance.'[22] Janik is referring to a reading of Weininger that maintains that, because of Weininger's method of argumentation, based on Kantian dialectics, his pitting of male and female, Jew and non-Jew, is somehow softened and made less consequential. While Janik's position is well argued, a complacent attitude toward the kind of contextualization he proposes presents its own specific dangers. First and foremost is the risk in creating a critical atmosphere that can function as an apology. The issues that Janik raises are of course similar to the ones raised in the previous chapter regarding how Lombroso should be read. It is important to avoid the pitfall of reading a text such as Lombroso's or Weininger's from a modern perspective that ignores contextualizing and understanding the historical period that produced such texts – but it is equally important not to be blinded by the god of contextualization to the point where the pernicious content and influence of such a text are ignored or explained away.

For example, the new science of positivism, with its anti-clerical views, would have colored Lombroso's views toward Judaism. Nineteenth-century liberalism, with its rejection of religion and its emphasis on social assimilation, would also have influenced a thinker like Lombroso; assimilationist theories of the Zionist Theodor Herzl might also have had an effect. Careful consideration of the logic and values Lombroso employs in his analysis of the Jews demonstrates that any possible apologistic stance a modern reader might take toward a text of this kind is difficult to justify, notwithstanding an appreciation of the historical and social context in which it was written. Even if one were to attempt to explain Lombroso's views through an analysis of the effects of liberalism and positivism on his thought, it is these two movements themselves that become tainted if their ideological structures contain such room for prejudice and the rejection of difference.[23]

The examination of Boas, Lombroso, and Weininger shows

that the problems of Jewish self-hatred and Jewish self-denial were widespread and intimately connected to the antisemitic atmosphere in Europe during the nineteenth and early twentieth centuries. The widely differing responses of these figures to the issue of their relationship to Judaism and to themselves argues against taking contextualization too far and using it as a way to exculpate authors from their prejudices. Boas suffered far more discrimination for being Jewish than did Lombroso, yet he demonstrates far less prejudice against Jews in his writings. It is clear that responses to prejudice are a highly individual matter.

The transmission of theories about difference and the interest of texts such as Lombroso's and Weininger's raise pertinent issues and are important to our understanding of what constitutes theories about cultural difference and the ways in which these theories are perpetrated. The reception of Weininger in Italy shows the influence of Lombroso and makes intelligible the response a Jewish critic, Giulio Augusto Levi, to the antisemitism in Weininger when reviewing his text.

In his *Weininger in Italia,* Alberto Cavaglion speaks of the influence of Lombroso in paving the way for the warm welcome given to Weininger's theories by a certain group of influential Florentine intellectuals.[24] In the first few years after his work became known in Italy, Weininger's misogyny was embraced – and his antisemitism, like that of Lombroso, overlooked. Weininger was 'discovered' by an Italian philosopher, Giovanni Vailati, who met him at a conference in Paris in 1900, later read his work in the original, and then started passing it among his colleagues in Florence who could read German. The text reached a broader audience when it was translated into Italian in 1912, but it was already known to the Italian intellectual community because of a series of articles on it that appeared in 1906 and 1910. Giuseppe Prezzolini, the well-known Florentine literary critic, wrote an article entitled 'Enemy of the Female' in 1906, which claimed that Weininger's *Sex and Character,* notwithstanding the title, was concerned with philosophical problems and was in fact anti-sexual. On February 10, 1910, *La Voce,* published in Florence under the direction of Prezzolini, dedicated a special issue to 'La questione sessuale.' In it Weininger's work was summarized, reviewed, and lauded as brilliant by Giulio Augusto Levi, another literary critic of the Florentine group. Levi's reaction to Weininger is emblematic of the stance of the *La Voce* critics: he summarizes many of Weininger's remarks on the inferiority of women, directly and unabashedly repeating the points that Weininger raises in his book. Yet on the subject of Jews in Weininger's theories, Levi, although Jewish himself, is almost mute. He dedicates only a short paragraph to this topic in his very long essay: 'In the chapter on Judaism, after having affirmed that the Jew completely lacks faith in himself and in the external world, he explains precisely how Christ could have been born out of Judaism, because 'the founder of religion is that man who has lived totally without God, and yet nonetheless has succeeded in winning faith.' Weininger without a doubt suffered from the radical uncertainty that he attributes to the Jew and wanted to win a faith.'[25]

Levi gives us very little information here about Weininger's writings concerning Jews: according to Weininger, the Jew lacked faith, and Judaism was the appropriate religion to produce Jesus. He concludes this abbreviated and quite misleading version with his own analysis of Weininger's conversion. Weininger, in fact, said much more than this about the Jew in the chapter on Judaism, as he attempted to undermine its history as a forerunner of Christianity by positing it as a kind of lowness that Jesus had to overcome in himself in order to become the founder of a new religion, the opposite of the old one.

This censorship and rewriting on Levi's part are telling. They characterize the relationship of this group of Italian critics to Weininger's text and demonstrate the willingness of a Jewish critic to overlook the most damaging part of Weininger's text in a move that can only be called self-denying.

Even the misogyny is diluted and downplayed, as Levi and later critics attempted to elevate Weininger to the status of genius without a full reckoning of the theories themselves. Levi tries to psychologize away the most disturbing part of Weininger's theories on Jews, as he thematizes Weininger's 'uncertainty.' In Levi's reaction we see a certain ambiguity about his own place in culture as he disclaims the importance of Weininger's self-hatred, the relation of that hatred to his philosophy, and the chilling implications of his theories for the continued existence of Judaism.

Other critics responded in a similar vein, excitedly discussing their reductive and self-serving version of Weininger's misogyny and ignoring the antisemitism. It was only in 1913 that Italian intellectuals would respond to the antisemitism of Weininger's text, and only through the impetus of a critic coming from outside Italy. In 1913, the French author André Spire wrote *Trois Juifs,* in which he confronts the question of Weininger's antisemitism. Once again it was the *La Voce* group who reviewed the text and spread word of it through Italy, and it was only after the publication of Spire's book that the question of antisemitism became an issue in the pages of *La Voce* and on the Italian scene in general.

The idiosyncratic history of the first stage of Weininger reception in Italy, full of truncations, blindness, and deviations, mimics the confused logic of the theories themselves. The visibility of difference, the ethics of critical blindness, and the nature of marginalization itself are central issues in a reading of the disassociation of the Jewish author – or Jewish critic, in the case of Levi – from a text on Jews. The reception of Weininger in Italy is thus plagued by the same problems that led to the text's inception: ambivalence, hostility, and self-abnegation on the part of the author as well as the critic receiving the text years later.

Many of the issues raised by a reading of Lombroso and Weininger are present in the works of the Neapolitan journalist and novelist Matilde Serao, a self-made woman who was well known for her antifeminism. Self-denial and its more extreme form, self-hatred, are not limited to Jews: they appear in every group stigmatized by marginalization, including women. As we will see in the chapters to come, concerns raised by a woman author who challenges the status of women while sundering herself from her sex are similar to those raised by a Jewish author who problematizes the status of the Jews in modern culture.

CHAPTER FIVE

MATILDE SERAO AND THE BODY OF PASSION

From Journalism to Fiction: Caught in the Canon

M atilde Serao holds a significantly underrepresented position in the canon of Italian letters today.[1] A well-known and respected journalist for more than forty years, she founded a Roman newspaper, *Il Corriere di Roma,* with her husband, Edoardo Scarfoglio. After their separation between 1902 and 1903, she started a newspaper in Naples, *Il Giorno,* on her own. A political conservative and a confirmed monarchist, she wrote many front-page editorials on political and social issues for these and other newspapers, penned fashion and travel columns, and was the author of more than forty volumes of stories and novels.

During her lifetime, Serao's literary reputation was held in high regard. Considered at the time a foremost practitioner of *verismo,* she often concentrated in both her literary and journalistic works on the slums of Naples. Many of her novels centered primarily on female characters whose lives are affected by their passions and whose fate in society is dictated by their gender. Her literary production was acclaimed not only for the *veristi* work, as we today might expect, but also for some of the novels that center on love, which were considered unusual and interesting.[2]

Critical prejudices about popular fiction that have grown up in the past fifty years have helped obfuscate interest in Serao's work for the modern reader.[3] Most critics from Croce on have artificially divided her literary output into two categories: the naturalistic works and the novels that are disparagingly called 'sentimental,' especially by those who champion her naturalistic vein.[4]

Serao's pluralistic literary production has served, together with critical prejudice, to marginalize her as an author of interest almost exclusively to feminist scholars reexamining the work of women writers and their place in the canon. The ironies and contradictions that surround the creation and subsequent loss of her literary reputation do not end here. For when we examine the renewed interest in Serao's work within the critical community and then compare her journalistic essays with her novels, the theme of contradiction itself stands out when it comes to her views about her own sex. Her perspective on the role of women in society and her proposed solutions to the problem of women's inequality put her into a category as yet not fully articulated or discussed by critics: that of a woman who is highly disparaging of her own gender, who like Lombroso and Weininger takes a problematic distance from her own identity.[5]

Serao's newspaper editorials concerning the lives of women are unabashedly prescriptive: they should be at the center of the home as mothers, wives, perhaps even writers. They should never be divorcées, voters, lawyers, or other professionals.[6] Serao's own life reflects an extraordinary level of paradox and ambivalence; her editorials speak out against divorce and spinsterhood, yet she left her husband and then lived with another man.[7] She opposed women's suffrage and advised women to stay out of public life, yet she built a career for herself as one of Italy's foremost journalists and the first woman to found a newspaper. Her self-empowerment and her continued support of the disenfranchisement of women form a puzzle whose pieces can be discovered only through a reading of both her journalistic and fictive works.

The issues surrounding any analysis of Serao's work are complex indeed. Most Serao criticism of the past twenty years has involved a debate over the possibility of reading her as a feminist or at least as having hidden 'feminist' tendencies.

Some have felt that, since some of her novels and editorials concentrate on the lives of working women and their deplorable working conditions, their content constitutes at least a sympathetic viewpoint to women's autonomy outside the home if not a feminist perspective on women's labor.[8] Lucienne Kroha, in her discussion of current criticism of several important women writers in the late nineteenth century such as Serao, Neera, Sibilla Aleramo, and the Marchese Colombo, has pointed out its limited aspects, identifying it as 'the tendency to read their work in the light of late twentieth-century ideological expectations, as more-or-less disappointing, unmediated documents of feminine oppression or feminist consciousness. Little or no attention is accorded to the novelty and complexity of their enterprise as women writing in the specific social and literary context of late nineteenth-century Italy, other than to point out that it may have interfered with their ability to take strong feminist positions.'[9] Kroha points out that Serao's contemporaries found her more onerous to classify than the others, a situation parodied by Luigi Verga's going so far as to call Serao a hermaphrodite in order to explain the difficulty of categorizing her.[10]

One critic has found a way of articulating what can be called feminist tensions in Serao's work while at the same time understanding the difference between the raising of such issues and claiming a specific political position. Ursula Fanning, in 'Sentimental Subversion: Representations of Female Friendships in the Work of Matilde Serao,' presents a convincing argument regarding the important role of female friendship in Serao's popular novels.[11] The complicated set of female protagonists found in her work lends itself well to this type of analysis, as Fanning draws out the intricate friendships and relationships between them and other female characters. Furthermore, their relationship to each other as women and their identity within society form an integral part of what makes them interesting today. In the texts Fanning analyzes, friendship between women either supplants or enriches heterosexual relations, which are seen as unfulfilling or unsat-isfactory. She concludes that 'Serao's presentation of female friendship must ultimately be recognized as undeniably politi-cal, *in spite of herself.* It functions as a challenge to specific institutions, including heterosexual marriage and patriarchal society as a whole.'[12]

Through this statement Fanning makes a crucial distinction between the effect of these friendships, in other words, how they can be read and understood, especially by readers today, and authorial intent. She also points to a set of contradictions and paradoxes within Serao's work regarding her views on women, since this purported affirmation of female friendship occurs 'in spite of herself.' What could the phrase 'in spite of herself' mean for an author like Serao? How does the position of political and personal ambivalence that this phrase implies manifest itself within the complex opus of Serao's multifac-eted literary and journalistic production?

The location and definition of woman for a woman writer raises some delicate issues. The concept of woman as other is, after all, defined by phallogocentrism: woman as *man's* other. I contend that Serao, as a woman writer, adopts what can be characterized as a patriarchal point of view toward woman while at the same time problematizing her margin-alized status. This simultaneous sensitivity to the issue of mar-ginalization for women and her own view of women as mar-ginalized provides a complex site of analysis, as we will see. A reading of some of Serao's 'love' novels, including her first novel, *Cuore infermo,* and two later ones, *Addio amore!* and its sequel, *Castigo,* brings to light some of the contradic-tions found in Serao's fictive world and demonstrates her am-bivalent position on women. In this chapter I discuss Serao's treatment of her female protagonists in these three novels, using Serao's constructs of passion and illness as an index to her views. I then turn to some of her journalistic writings to examine the ambivalence toward women found there and to look at the ways in which her journalism clarifies some of the

84

questions and concerns that an examination of a writer like Serao brings to light.[13]

At Passion's Door

S erao's 'love' novels employ the effect of passion as a central theme. In some of these novels, the female protagonists are trapped by their emotions as they fall prey to a passion that is usually unrequited or unfulfilling. In this way, passion can even take on a physical dimension as the character falls ill and expresses bodily symptoms of sickness. Ultimately, it functions as an indication of the difficult status of woman and serves to establish her precise identity.[14]

Cuore infermo, Serao's first novel, provides an interesting case study of the relationship of female characters to passion.[15] The text is a fascinating and well-constructed blend of the tragic story of Beatrice and of observations on the aristocratic life-style in Naples during the last part of the nineteenth century. Beatrice, as a young woman, has resolved to avoid completely any expression of emotion in her life after the early childhood trauma of her mother's death. Her mother's demise came as a result of a weak heart that could not withstand the emotional demands of love. Beatrice has guarded her knowledge of the cause of her mother's death from everyone around her, including her father. In a confrontation with him, when he accuses her of indifference toward her husband, Beatrice tells him the secret of her mother's illness: 'She loved and was quiet: her heart said to her: I am sick, I cannot stand all this, I will die of it – and she quieted even this voice. . . . [S]ometimes at night, when her anxieties mounted, the beat of her heart became rapid, her breathing became troubled, her face ashen, her hands swelled. . . . [T]hey say that she received with grace the woman for whom she was betrayed, that she even kissed her.'[16]

Thus, we discover that her father's betrayal of her mother, along with her unrequited love for him, caused her early death. As a result of this knowledge, Beatrice has become cold, calm, and aloof because she is afraid that she has inherited her mother's weak heart; as she tells her father, 'These illnesses of the heart are inherited, like tuberculosis and madness.'[17] The illnesses to which she compares this heart disease are revealing: tuberculosis furnishes a site of analysis in itself, as does insanity. Neither, of course, is necessarily hereditary. Susan Sontag, in 'Illness as Metaphor,' describes tuberculosis in the nineteenth century as 'encumbered by the trappings of metaphor. . . . The fantasies inspired by TB in the last century, by cancer now, are responses to a disease thought to be intractable and capricious.'[18] Cardiac disease, on the other hand, 'implies a weakness, trouble, failure that is mechanical; there is no disgrace, nothing of the taboo that once surrounded people afflicted with TB.'[19] Beatrice's comparison of these diseases thus causes the image of heart disease to be invested, contaminated as it were, with the same kind of connotations inspired by tuberculosis and insanity, one physical in origin but mysterious and capricious, the other thought at the time to be entirely emotional. We may argue that Beatrice's particular manifestation of heart disease takes on the symptoms of tuberculosis; as Sontag describes it, 'TB is understood as a disease of extreme contrasts: white pallor and red flush, hyperactivity alternating with languidness . . . febrile activity, passionate resignation.'[20] Beatrice undergoes moments of a flushed face and also pallor,[21] and her behavior shifts erratically from passive to active; it can be read as symptoms of the very disease that her heart disease is not. As Sontag remarks, 'the TB-prone character that haunted imaginations in the nineteenth century was an amalgam of two different fantasies: someone both passionate and repressed.'[22] Here the characteristics of tuberculosis have been metaphorically displaced onto the activity of passionate behavior for Beatrice, as she shows both a strongly repressed side until she admits her love for Marcello and an equally strong passionate side that then emerges.

What is particularly interesting about this transfer in meaning is that it works simultaneously on several levels. The displacement of tuberculosis to the sick heart functions as a metaphor for women and love. Symptoms are also presented of a disease that has as its physical target the essential symbol of love, the heart. To complicate matters further, it is clearly emotion, and not, for example, physical activity, that brings on the signs of a heart in trouble and causes the demise of those women so afflicted.[23]

Beatrice marries Marcello, a member of another Neapolitan aristocratic family, not out of love but because it is expected that she will marry. Marcello falls deeply in love with her after the wedding, and when she refuses to share any intimacy with him, including the disclosure of the secret of her weak heart, he turns to another woman, Lalla D'Aragona.

Lalla is mourning her husband, who expired as a result of too much sexual and emotional passion for her after a brief and intense marriage. The portrait of the 'other woman' is a telling one; Lalla is depicted as a kind of stereotypical modern woman, as Beatrice is warned by her father about her: 'She is really the modern woman, the passionate woman, strange, possibly superficial, delicate, ill, nervous, capricious, of different appearances that seduce everyone; a woman made to please the restless and refined modern youth.'[24]

Lalla is figured as the personification of illness; she is always suffering from an undisclosed sickness. The connection between the definition of a modern woman and illness is made clear in Beatrice's father's description of Lalla as *ammalata*. Lalla and Marcello begin a love triangle that includes Beatrice as an absent yet primary object of love. Lalla is obsessed with her, not because she is Marcello's wife and he is in love with her, but for what are outlined as both masochistic and perverse reasons. Marcello, on the other hand, plays the part of the spurned lover who stays with Lalla because of her obsession with Beatrice: 'Their strange love had begun in the name of Beatrice, she far away. For unhealthy pleasure, Lalla enjoyed throwing it often in Marcello's face, like a blow of a whip, in the highest moment of passion. She enjoyed it immensely, because she herself felt in her heart the backlash of that pain.'[25]

Lalla's modernity is both her inspiration, as she rejects another suitor, unmarried and clearly more suitable, in favor of this perverse love for Marcello, and her undoing, as her modernity translates as masochism, illness, and suffering. Beatrice eventually becomes jealous of Lalla and undergoes a sensual reawakening that expresses itself through an obsession with the sight and smell of exotic flowers. At first puzzled by this sensuality, she finally understands its cause and purpose when she sees a picture of lovers kissing, and she then confesses her love to her husband. He gladly abandons his love-hate relationship with Lalla and returns to Beatrice, and they spend several delirious months enjoying their love – until Beatrice's heart gives out and she quite literally drops dead.

The three main characters in this novel all suffer deeply as a result of passion. They each, however, respond differently to its demands. Lalla feeds off passion in order to sustain unhealthy relationships, Marcello suffers from passion for Beatrice but is perversely able to express it through a masochistic relationship with Lalla, and Beatrice both lives and dies from passion as it first animates her and then causes her heart to swell and stop. The novel is sophisticated in its subtle rendering of these characters' relationships to one another and in its exploration of the tense kinship of love and hatred in Marcello and Lalla's affair.

Cuore infermo, as Serao's first novel, can be seen as a model for her later works in which passion remains a central focus. For both Beatrice and Lalla, it takes on a physical form manifested through bodily symptoms. The relation between what Beatrice calls '*il cuore fisico*' [the physical heart] and '*il cuore psichico*' [the psychic heart] is a complicated one here. The paranomastic rendering indicates that it is not the possible stress of love that causes Beatrice's latent heart disease to man-

ifest itself, it is rather emotion itself. Love is figured as a physically generative force, capable of causing the heart to swell
both figuratively and materially. In some of Serao's later fiction, she takes the somatization of the social and emotional
results of passion for women even further than this. Note also
that, while Marcello as well suffers because of love, he does
not express it through his body, as Beatrice, her mother, and
Lalla all do.

Serao's 1890 novel, *Addio amore!,* is a story of the passions
of a young aristocratic woman, Anna. At the beginning of the
novel she is planning to elope with Giustino, her socially un-
suitable suitor. She and her sister Laura, both orphans, are in
the care of Cesare, their legal guardian. After Cesare stops the
elopement, Anna literally becomes ill with her passion, developing a strange illness in which all her blood rushes to the
surface of her body. During her convalescence from the passion *and* from passion's illness she becomes enamored of Cesare himself, described as a cold, cynical, ladies' man, who
does not return her affection. Anna falls into a deep depressed
lethargy and begins to forecast her own death as a result of her
unrequited love. To save her from death, Cesare reluctantly
marries her after she agrees to give him his complete freedom.

After the marriage, Anna becomes even more a slave to her
passion. Literally inscribing the name of Cesare on her body,
she wears a relic holder around her neck in which she has
placed two notes from him, and on her arm she wears six thin
bracelets, each with a letter of his name. Her passion has
become an inscriptive compulsion that plays itself out bodily.

Cesare promptly falls in love with Anna's seemingly cold
and distant sister Laura, described as similar to Cesare in tem-
perament. In the meantime Anna herself gets a suitor; Luigi, a
friend of Cesare's, falls deeply in love with her. From behind a
curtain Anna witnesses a romantic encounter between her
husband and her sister. She confronts her sister, who confesses
her love for Cesare, and then confronts Cesare, who tells her
she is mad and tries to explain away the passionate kisses and

exclamations that she has seen and overheard. Anna, uncon-
vinced, goes to Luigi's house and commits suicide at the end of
the novel.

The primary locus of sexual difference in *Addio amore!*,
passion goes beyond the parameters of self-control, as it is
blamed as the cause of other physical problems. As the nar-
rator of *Addio amore!* tells us after Anna almost dies of
'passion':

> There is no actual fatal disease that is called passion: ancient
> and modern doctors don't recognize it, have never found it,
> in their autopsy of the cadaver. But passion is such a subtle
> deceiver that she is at the base of all fatal diseases. She is in
> tuberculosis that makes those who love too much or who
> were not loved enough agonize for years; she is in heart
> disease, in that heart which expands under the wave of emo-
> tional passion, which closes up in desperation; she is in long-
> term anemia which destroys the human body, fiber by fiber,
> icing the skin, shattering all energy; she is in the neurosis
> which makes one shiver with cold and burn in unbearable
> heat, which attacks the brain or the stomach, which makes
> teeth chatter with a deadly cold and which convulses all the
> nerves in a cramp which makes one crazy. . . . [O]ne doesn't
> die of tuberculosis, of anemia, of hypertrophy, of neuro-
> sis . . . one dies, really, for one single reason.[26]

In *Addio amore!*, as in *Cuore infermo*, it is specifically the
female body that bears the signs of passion. Expressed not
only physically but medically as well, it is posited as the site
of ailments, the mysterious shifting and displacing cause of
'hard' disease. It is also capable of creating diseases of its own,
as we see from this description of the mysterious fever and
bodily signs that assailed Anna after her failed elopement:

> On the third day the red marks on the cheeks and on the
> temples became a bright red: on the neck, on the hands, on
> the arms fiery red spots appeared. . . . [I]n short the whole
> skin had these spots and 'red fever' showed itself in all its
> vehemence. This is to say that the blood, which was too rich,

too ardent, too impetuous, had so greatly stressed the tissues of the veins that all the boiling blood had come up under the surface. . . . [O]n the sixth day those spots swelled up and became blackish . . . broke the skin in several places, and let erupt a blackish blood. . . . Anna seemed to spit blood, seemed to cry blood; it seemed that her hands, tortured like those of Jesus, seeped blood.[27]

In this passage there is a specific illness cited, that of *la febbre purpurea,* or 'red' fever. The color red, *porpora,* evoked here, further suggests *la scarlattina* [scarlet fever]. This illness described above does in fact correspond to symptoms of scarlet fever, up to a certain point: it begins as a sore throat, which then turns red, and a red rash spreads from the face to the rest of the body on approximately the third day of illness, just as Serao describes here. But on the sixth day of the sickness in the text, there is a dramatic change, as the bleeding – which is not symptomatic of scarlet fever – begins. As Anna's symptoms change, another illness is evoked through paronomastic association: puerperal fever, *la febbre della puerpera,* usually known as childbirth fever.

The association *purpurea/puerpera* suggests more than a change of illness; it marks gender on Anna's disease. Puerperal fever in a literal sense is the result of fruit-bearing passion, but here the terms are reversed: Anna has not given birth; she has been thwarted in love.[28]

What looks like a simple literalization here (e.g., scarlet fever equals red equals blood) is actually a complicated passage from the description of an illness to an array of symbolic meanings. Passion is expressed through illness, and this malady is very specifically gendered. Furthermore, in the description of passion as the cause of all disease, it is personified as 'a subtle deceiver.' This naming goes beyond a simple linguistic gendering as passion is made into an active agent that tricks doctors and pathologists in order to wreak its damage through physical signs of illness that kill the body.[29]

In the passage above, these bodily manifestations of passion become a sign of suffering, which in turn becomes metaphorically and literally associated with stigmata. The first suffering figure here is that of the wounded woman. At the end of the passage, another is denoted as Anna's hands are compared to those of Jesus ['come quelle di Gesù']. Two kinds of stigmata are simultaneously evoked, first, the wounds of Jesus, and second, the spontaneous bleeding from the skin, often associated with hysteria.

The passage is metaphorically rich. Medically speaking, the bleeding is a description of the pathological definition of stigmata, but the comparison of Anna's hands with those of Jesus thereby shifts the definition from the pathological to the religious. The evocation of a religious figure creates an important change of scene, serving to both displace the suffering figure and to transform the meaning of its expression, the blood. The meaning of Anna's blood is shifted to a symbolic arena in which bloodied hands signify a tortured suffering and in which gender is not an issue. The danger of her bleeding being associated with a womanly bleeding is thus avoided. And Anna's suffering for love is transferred to a higher plane, in which the banality of the situation (i.e., 'teenager tries to elope, is caught, and pines away') is masked.

The first meaning given for *passione* in the Zingarelli Italian dictionary is 'bodily suffering, pain, or physical torment – of Jesus Christ, suffering, or death of Jesus.' The term is entrenched in Christian theology, as it crosses the borders between physical suffering, religious martyrdom, and emotional love. Serao uses *passione* to describe Anna's fate at the hands of love, and the reversion to a religious source of suffering and martyrdom is highly significant, as the move from suffering woman to martyr is accomplished by the end of the passage.

This displacement is important in another way as well. In the Marian cult, the figure of the virgin martyr is particularly important in the establishment of an 'ideal' role for women. This model ends up in a negation of the female, as we see in the following passage from Marina Warner: 'Theologians like

Cyprian (d 258) and Tertullian and Jerome appeal to women to adopt the virginal life because then they will not have to suffer the consequences of the Fall. . . . [T]o some extent, virginity thus reversed the Fall. Jerome wrote: "As long as a woman is for birth and children, she is different from man as body is from soul. But when she wishes to serve Christ more than the world, then she will cease to be a woman, and will be called man." '[30]

The shift from wounded woman to Jesus neatly avoids questions of gendering, as it shies away from an association or interpretation of Anna's blood as menstrual in nature.[31] Yet the notion of the virgin martyr carries with it a gendered meaning: she loses her female gender, as the Christian tradition that Warner cites associates what is womanly with female bodily functions, a distinctly pre-Freudian 'biology as destiny' argument. The path to martyrdom is one that encourages fasting until the onset of menarche, in other words, a loss of that which signifies sexual difference. Anna's bleeding thus becomes a way in which to lose gender and gain the kind of credibility to which only a tortured religious figure can aspire, a figure whose suffering replaces sexuality with a higher ideal of suffering for religious passion.[32] Through the crossover effected by the simile of the hands, two definitions of passion and two meanings of stigmata are made indistinct in this passage and indeed are merged at the end.

The identification of passion with illness is complicated by the fact that Anna was suffering from a fever, which we can surmise was the first sign of her malady, as she prepared for the elopement. The stage was thus set for the disease that assailed her after the disappointment of the failed escape. The inability to recognize this symptom as disease until after the dramatic scene of the discovery had taken place casts an interesting light on the seemingly reversible cause-and-effect relationship of passion and illness. Was illness not truly illness until passion had been disappointed? Was the disease not in fact caused by the emotions of the thwarted elopement but instead grounded in the empirical world of germs and bacteria that had already been breeding in Anna's physiological system? If passion can generate a malady, or at the very least facilitate its recognition, can illness in turn generate passion? It is important to keep in mind that it is only after this great illness that Anna becomes enamored of Cesare.

Rather than die from this passion-induced malady, Anna recovers in order to live and then love again; her death comes instead because she wills it and then stages it at her suitor's house, an end designed to avenge her own wounded honor as much as possible by making it appear that she was Luigi's lover. On the one hand, Anna's manifestation of suffering is passive and somatic; on the other hand, she later takes charge of the situation and orchestrates her own end. The tension created between these two approaches characterizes the ambivalences and ambiguities we see in the novel regarding the role of the female protagonists.

Passion is what separates Serao's female characters from the male characters: only the female characters are capable of dying for love. Passion is not only capable of undoing the body that bears its stigmata, it can also be inscribed on the body, as in the case of Anna's wearing of Cesare's name and his writings like holy yet secular relics. These effects on Anna serve as a commentary on the identity of woman for Serao, as it establishes the female as a passive vehicle for illness.

Passion simultaneously creates the figure of woman and undoes Serao's textual characters. Yet they are not simple, passive constructions of woman as other, characters who are spoken or spoken for; they are instead articulate, speaking subjects. Some of the passages in which Anna expresses her feelings for Cesare and analyzes the nature of love are among the most eloquent and poetic sections of the novel. Anna is not the typical love-stricken heroine who slowly wastes away: her decision to commit suicide is based on a cold summary of the facts, and she herself actively ends her life. Even her passion-induced illness is a dramatic one as she bursts and bleeds.

94

Lombroso, it will be recalled, had his own views regarding the effect of passion on women, views that are not at odds with the way Serao treated the issue:

> We saw that for women love is a kind of slavery accepted with enthusiasm, a sacrifice of all of herself made disinterestedly for the lover . . . Pure and great passion by itself leads the enamored woman more toward suicide or insanity than toward crime; if it leads to crime this is a sign that she was able to unleash a latent base of evil, or that the virility of her character gave to her vehement passions means for crime that a really female woman would never commit. The real crime therefore for the passion of love is in the woman – if you can call this a crime – suicide: other crimes are nothing but hybrid forms.[33]

There is a strong correlation in this passage between the way in which Lombroso articulated his analysis of women in love as willing victims to a system that somehow lies beyond their control and Serao's fictive characters. The similarity between Lombroso and Serao regarding the reaction to and effect of passion is not surprising, since both showed sympathy for women to a certain point. The fact that Lombroso proposed suicide as the only 'feminine' form of 'crime' for love follows stereotypes prevalent at the time regarding women's passivity. That Serao was affected by these same characterizations seems clear, but she also questioned this state of affairs in her novels.

Castigo the sequel to *Addio amore!*, (1893), is the story of Cesare and Laura's guilt after Anna's suicide. As they grapple with their complicated feelings toward Anna and each other, another female protagonist, the duchess of Cleveland, Lady Hermione, mysteriously appears on the scene. What is striking about this character is that she is a dead ringer for Anna. Luigi immediately transfers all his unrequited love for Anna to this stranger. Cesare, who has been looking for Luigi to challenge him to a duel to avenge his honor, sees Hermione, follows her believing she is Anna's ghost, and discovers that

Luigi has been courting her. Doubly inflamed by jealousy as well as by his offended honor, Cesare meets Luigi for a duel and wounds him. Cesare continues to follow Hermione, obsessed with her resemblance to his dead wife and smitten with rather tardy feelings of love for Anna.

Both Luigi and Cesare want to use Hermione as a vehicle for their frustrated passions for the dead Anna. Hermione, a strange and mysterious character in her own right, is presented as an independent, idiosyncratic woman who frequently refers to death and past lives, thus creating some doubt as to her earthly status. She falls in love with Luigi, but when she realizes that he only loves her for her resemblance to Anna, she escapes from him and Italy on her private yacht.

Anna, in *Addio amore!,* is the victim of her passions. The continuation of the novel in its sequel can be read as a rewriting of this female passivity. Laura, Anna's stronger younger sister, marries the irresistible Cesare herself a few months after Anna's death. She is seemingly better able to manage the situation; even though Cesare is no longer interested in her love because he is consumed by guilt over Anna's fate, Laura patiently and cleverly follows him in his search for Luigi. Unlike Anna, she exploits moments of passivity and action as instruments to control her relationship with Cesare. It is in the appearance of Hermione, however, that Anna as the failed victim of passion is vindicated and her story rewritten. Hermione is everything that Anna was not: she is able to entirely control her passion, she travels alone, she is married but lives apart from her husband. She has her own means of transportation that allow her to come and go as she pleases, even from one country to another. Hermione's character is used to work out the passion that Cesare and Luigi both still maintain for Anna, but she does not fall victim to it, and she refuses to be Anna's double. As she says to Luigi just before her departure, 'You don't love Hermione Darlington, why do you call her? Goodbye, Luigi . . . your woman is in the tomb . . . you can only love Anna and she is dead, she's dead: you can only love her, in remembering the past, in the tomb. . . . [T]he only thing that remains is to open up the chapel of the Dias family and to go to sleep in the tomb of Anna, like Hamlet. This is what is left for you: go, go, goodbye.'[34]

Anna is marginalized in *Addio amore!* as the two characters closest to her, Cesare and Laura, neither understand nor tolerate her emotions. These figures are described as similar; she is described as different. Anna is often referred to after her death as 'the other,' the one whom Hermione resembles, the one whom Laura and Cesare feel too guilty to discuss.[35]

In *Castigo*, Anna is in a sense recentered in the world of female protagonists who gain some control over their destiny through the appearance of Hermione. She could thus be viewed as an ideal refiguration of Anna, one that would allow her to live again, to regain a central position in the novel. Precisely because Hermione is not herself a passive victim of love, however, this reworking is not possible. The irony here is that Hermione refuses this role; however, were she to accept it, Anna's passivity would not be vindicated, it would merely be mirrored and the chain of female victims of love would go on.

In *Fantasia*, Serao's 1883 novel of two schoolgirls' friendship and the eventual betrayal of one by the other, Lucia the deserter is allowed to get away with her crime and Caterina, the victim, self-destructs at the end of the text. In her analysis of *Fantasia*, Kroha says the following: 'It is clear that though Serao does identify with Caterina morally and at the deeper meta-literary level, she does not believe in her as a character any more than she does in Lucia. . . . Serao can endorse neither her story nor her characters, but can come up with no convincing alternatives.'[36]

The question of why Serao would abandon certain types of female characters to a difficult fate is also pertinent in *Castigo* to our understanding of the relationships between Serao's female protagonists and her views on women. In *Castigo*, Serao shipwrecked her female characters: Hermione, the somewhat liberated woman, drowns in the end on her yacht, the vehicle of her freedom, Anna has already killed herself in *Addio amore!*, and Laura is left abandoned, after her husband Cesare is killed by Luigi in their final duel. The character of Anna does not work successfully since she is a passive victim of love, Laura is the cold-hearted betrayer of her sister, and Hermione's freedom is shown to be risky and is ultimately her undoing. Kroha's statement regarding *Fantasia* would seem to hold true for these novels as well, as no acceptable alternatives to these unhappy endings are offered.

In her fiction Serao creates many different types of female characters, from the passive to the active, from working women to aristocratic convalescents. The confusion and ambivalence we see in the roles they play are mirrored in Serao's biography, in which her own centralized status is dependent on her complicated relationship to the ideal society she describes and prescribes to her female readership. To Serao, the other works as a figure of displacement to the notion of the 'ideal' woman who could be happy in a patriarchal society. Serao's fictional world is a complicated, shifting construction in which her female protagonists play out the ambivalences, contradictions, and difficulties of modern society.

The juxtaposition of Serao's journalistic writings about women as real subjects with her novelistic treatment of them raises some interesting questions of what the world of fiction held for her. The occasionally utopian manipulation of her female characters and their partial but ambiguous empowerment within the 'safe' world of fiction offers endless and fascinating possibilities of interpretation. The case of Serao as a writer divided over her own identity is not unique. However, the question of a woman writer with potentially misogynist views, especially one who concentrates on the situation of women in society, is one that has not been adequately addressed by criticism. Andrea Dworkin discusses the appeal that the right holds for some in *Right-Wing Women* but does not discuss female misogyny as such; in fact, there is a kind of apology made for figures like Anita Bryant and Marabel Morgan through an analysis of the kind of emotional and physical security the right holds for them.[37]

I do not mean to suggest that there is necessarily a connection between female misogyny and right-wing or conservative politics. We can see, however, that what was at stake in feminist politics at the end of the nineteenth century, when battles about women's suffrage were heating up, is hardly in line with the kind of political conservatism that Serao demonstrated throughout her career, especially concerning the role of women. A notable exception to her conservatism is her anti-Fascist stance adopted early on during the Mussolini regime, which literary historians agree cost her the Nobel Prize in literature at the same time that Fascist censorship was ruining her newspaper. Some of the criteria that Dworkin applies to Right-wing women in order to understand their political allegiances can, I believe, be applied to Serao as well. As the lone female figure on the journalistic front in Italy at the end of the century, she was surrounded by domineering male figures such as Gabriele D'Annunzio and Edoardo Scarfoglio. One could speculate that it might have been easier for Serao to pretend she was 'one of the boys' than to explore in depth her connection to other women and to the female condition. As Dworkin remarks on a contemporary right-wing figure, 'Phyllis Schlafly, the Right's not-born-again philosopher of the absurd, is apparently not having a hard time. She seems possessed by Machiavelli, not Jesus. It appears that she wants to be The Prince. She might be viewed as that rare woman of any ideological persuasion who really does see herself as one of the boys, even as she claims to be one of the girls.'[38] Speculation is once again tempting: If Phyllis Schlafly were to become a novelist, what would her female characters be like?

In another assessment of the relationship of a woman writer to her text, Mary Shelley's *Frankenstein*, Barbara Johnson demonstrates how the story can be read as deeply ambivalent toward parenting and addresses the issue of contradiction in a woman's life. As she discusses the author's attitudes regarding the creation of the monster, Johnson highlights an interesting aspect of this ambivalence, applicable, I believe, to Serao as well: 'While the story of a man who is haunted by his own contradictions is representable as an allegory of monstrous doubles, how indeed would it have been possible for Mary to represent feminine contradiction from the point of view of its repression otherwise than precisely in the gap between angels of domesticity and an uncompleted monsteress, between the murdered Elizabeth and the dismembered Eve?'[39]

Johnson claims that the 'power of feminine contradiction,' as she later calls it, provides a solution for the problem of female authority in the text. Contradiction is at once a vehicle for this authority and at the same time an analysis of the source of its power; this dual characteristic sums up very well the situation in which we find Serao. Just as her many female characters express different aspects of and responses to their entrapment within society, critics of Serao have erred when they overly categorize her work, insist on consistency, and do not allow her the play and tension of contradiction. Seeing it instead as a positive attribute as Johnson does allows us to more fully understand and appreciate the rich complexity of Serao's work. It furthermore highlights the idea that her lack of consistency in her female characters can be read as a potent statement.

Examining some of Serao's editorials on women allows us another opportunity to understand the meaning of contradiction in her writing. In these, Serao is not content with merely dictating the place of women as passive, nonvoting home-makers. She sometimes goes as far as demonstrating disdain and contempt for women concerning suffrage and feminism. The following passage, taken from an editorial she published in her own newspaper, *Il Giorno,* in 1925 shows clearly why it can be hard to conceive of her as any kind of feminist at all. The article, 'Ma che fanno le femministe?' [But What Are the Feminists Doing?], mocked women's intellectual capacity and jeered at the constituency for whom the feminists were at-tempting to obtain the vote:

> Have you ever considered, oh suffragists, that the majority of women are crassly ignorant? Have you ever considered that this large number of ignorant women do nothing to diminish their ignorance, they don't read a newspaper, open a book, they are only interested in conversations that come out of gossip? Have you ever considered that these feminine masses are impermeable to ideas and to knowledge, that they flee from thinking, from reflecting, and from judging? Look out, suffragists, if you want to explain to them local and statewide law . . . as they do in the kindergartens, with children, teach them a little summarizing lesson, and then make them repeat it. A kind of catechism, tit for tat.[40]

Serao's argument is clearly misogynistic. She forestalls po-tential objections and explanations for what she calls the ignorance of women, including their 'lack of opportunity,' by claiming that they do not want to alleviate their lack of knowledge, even with the tools of education laid out before them. She then resorts to an old favorite in the arsenal of misogynist weapons, asserting the incapacity of women to think and to reflect. A recipe for practice follows this Wein-ingerian cliché, as she claims that repetition is the only way to teach women the law. There is also an explicit and disturbing comparison of women to small children, who also learn by the same rote method.

This curiously equivocal story regarding Serao's views to-ward women does not end here. In other editorials she con-demned the working condition of telegraph operators, a job she herself held briefly as a young girl. She staunchly sup-ported women writers, but not most other professions for women.[41] Yet in some of her writings, such as the one I quote below, she shows such strong sympathy for women that it is hard to label her an 'antifeminist': indeed, the viability of such a term is called into question.

Serao is both the threatening monsteress who questions the

status of women, *in spite of herself,* and the would-be angel of domesticity, who feels that women had better just quietly make the most of their fate, that is, an unhappy existence in a society not set up in their favor. She recognizes the difficulty of her own enterprise and the existence of the patriarchal establishment in a 1901 article on maternity in *Il Mattino:* 'I know, as do many other women, that as the laws of modern society are written, there is no happiness possible for a woman, in whatever condition she finds herself: neither in marriage, nor in free love, nor in illicit love . . . and I also know, as do many other women, that everything should be changed in society, in the hearts of men and in human matters . . . and I know that no one will change everything and so thus it is not worth changing anything.'[42] Serao's conclusion, after her eloquent summation of the position of women in society, their limited opportunities, and the futility of change, is that they should dedicate themselves to the happiness of their families. This view is not so much a proclamation of any absolute value of self-sacrificing motherhood over independence but rather a cynical assessment of the available options and a refusal to revolt because of the impossibility of changing 'everything.'

Her bitter and defeatist attitude shows Serao's ability to be brutally honest about what women in her time faced and what their possibilities were. Is this the statement of a woman who thought that men and women were treated equally? It is obviously not. It is certainly not the statement of a woman willing to fight for better conditions for women – but only, it would seem, because she feels it would be futile, so stacked are the odds against women. Do the recognition of the difficulties for women and her simultaneous acceptance of this fate make her a 'feminist manqué'? Or, to use a highly charged word in our post-Holocaust era, a collaborator instead? Does her disparaging attitude toward women's ability to handle the vote intelligently mean that she believes in the intrinsic inferiority of women, or is she rather angered by women who do not try harder to raise themselves above the level of ignorance in which their society has left them? Where does one draw the line between what could easily and perhaps too simplistically be categorized as self-hatred or misogyny and an embittered but honest reckoning of precisely those conditions generated by inequality? The questions posed by Serao's positions on women bring to mind the discourse of 'Jewish self-hatred' discussed in the previous chapter. Various gendered, racial, or religious manifestations of 'self-hatred,' or rather its nuances, share common characteristics. The same problems that occur with the too-easy labeling of Jewish self-hatred manifest themselves here in simply calling Serao a misogynist woman.

As was the case with Lombroso, even more tensions surrounding the meaning and problems of marginalization emerge in Serao's work when another outsider group is introduced. In the next chapter I will discuss how Serao's view of woman as marginalized is played off against the more fully marginalized and scapegoated figure of the Jew found in some of her fiction.

CHAPTER SIX

WHO IS THE OTHER? THE CASE OF THE DIS-PLACED MARGIN

We have seen in the previous chapter how the body of the female character in Serao's love novels is used to express symptoms of passion through the illness it generates. Passion indicates helplessness on the part of the protagonist through a loss of autonomy. The lack of control signals larger problems for female characters in Serao's fictive world and for the women she writes about in the world of journalism as well. The identity of woman for Serao is unstable, as different kinds of female characters are displayed in her texts and diverse solutions to the problems caused by marginalization are attempted. That women are marginalized for Serao is self-evident: what is not so clear is the precise nature of their marginalization, as Serao's ambivalence about her own gender plays a role in her rendition of what liminality means. As we saw in the previous chapter, the difficult position of women in society was noted by Serao in her editorials. An analogy can be made to the situation of her female protagonists through their frequent attempts to gain autonomy just as they are prevented from doing so by the ideological construct Serao identifies as passion.

One way of attempting to reconcile marginality is to shift the margins: a disguise of liminality effected by changing its very coordinates. Sander Gilman analyzes the creation and functioning of stereotypes in *Difference and Pathology*, as he remarks, 'Stereotypes are a crude set of mental representations of the world. They are palimpsests on which the initial bipolar representations are still vaguely legible. They perpetuate a needed sense of difference between the "self" and the "object," which becomes the "Other." Because there is no real line between self and Other, an imaginary line must be drawn.'[1]

Gilman's analysis emphasizes the notion of drawing a line, setting up boundaries that must exist between the self and the world. Stereotypes function in two important ways here: first to establish these boundaries and second to make them exploitable for shifting blame away from the self and onto someone else. A strategy of scapegoating, it serves to focus attention on another person or group in order to push wrongdoing away from the center and out to the margins, just as the biblical priest lay his hands on the goat's head, put upon him all the sins of the people of Israel, and sent him away into the wilderness, away from civilization, away from the center.

This archetypal move of displacement can be implemented in another way through the creation of a distraction to disguise the margins, thus masking what is central and what is not. Serao adopts a similar strategy in an early story of hers and in a novel written approximately twenty-seven years later. The focus on the problem of marginalization remains constant, but the technique for dealing with it changes.

The case of a shifting margin appears in Serao's early *verista* story, 'Telegrafi dello stato' [State Telegraph Office], which was published in 1886.[2] The story treats the lives of young female telegraph operators who work for the government for very low wages. It begins as a day in the life of Maria Vitale, whose impoverished familial conditions are highlighted when we learn that the family has no clock or watch. The lack of convenient technology results in Maria's inadvertently leaving her house one hour earlier than necessary for work on this particular day and in the subsequent hardship. Portraits such as this are given of many of the other operators, as Serao concentrates on drawing their lives against the technological backdrop of the telegraph office, a space dominated by the electric charge and incessant clatter of the machines. The focus in the story soon shifts from Maria to that of the ambience of the telegraph office and the relationship of the characters to their work.

One character in particular is described as strange and marginalized, for whom the others cannot even describe their antipathy:

> In the large salon, Cristina Juliano arrived, said hello to them, without stopping. She appeared to be an ugly man dressed as a woman, with her large ruined body, too wide in the shoulders, too long in the torso, without hips, with large hands, knobby wrists, and huge feet. She still wore a summery white straw hat, pulled down on her forehead in order to soften the fright of her white, fearful crossed eye: and to uncover the wondrous abundance of two thick black braids, an overflowing richness of hair, which pulled her head backward from its weight.[3]

This judgmental and prescriptive description is presented as the reason for the other operators' avoidance of this woman/man. Juliano is described as too much of one thing (too wide in the shoulders, etc.) and not enough of another. It is not just that she lacks feminine characteristics (she is 'without hips'): she presents overtly masculine ones, which the text tells us about immediately, as it labels her 'an ugly man dressed as a woman.' Her large hands, knobby wrists, and enormous feet merely emphasize what we already know: this woman is not physically acceptable as such. Just in case there is any doubt about her physical unacceptability, the text shifts strategy in the next line, informing us that she is still wearing a summer hat even though it is no longer summer. Fashion and practicality are comingled as we find out that she wears this hat so as to hide her frightening crossed eye; an androgynous appearance gives way to monstrous qualities ('the fright of her white, fearful crossed eye'). The presence of Juliano problematizes not only what is male and what is female. It announces as well how the other characters react to messages about gender identification. Juliano serves as a warning as to what is acceptable for the woman worker, as she does not fit into any tolerable category.

The recounting of monstrous elements is continued by the description of Juliano's hair. In its almost frightening excessiveness, her female sexual characteristics, lacking in some respects, are presented as simultaneously out of proportion and out of control. She pays a price for the superfluous amount of hair, which unnaturally pulls her head back by its weight. Lombroso's view of the female criminal provides an interpretive frame through which part of the physical description of Juliano may be read. According to Lombroso, the female criminal usually displays physical signs of virility, such as broad shoulders and a 'masculine' jaw. Even more significant is the sign of too much hair, as he claims that female criminals often are hairier, which he also associates with virility, and demonstrate less baldness than 'normal' women. Prostitutes too display signs of virility, which mark them as something other than 'real' women. The signs of degeneration present in this description of Juliano point to a cultural stereotype of unacceptable woman made current by Lombroso's theories.

Juliano occasionally appears in the story among the other workers. The categorization of her as socially and physically outcast sets the stage for another even more marginalized woman, whose presence in the story becomes known only through what is viewed by the others as a cowardly act on her part. When a crisis arises as the government requests that on election day the workers put in extra hours or even entire shifts without pay, the operators rebel among themselves, but on the fateful day when the sign-up register is put before them, they fold under pressure and agree to the extra work. The first person to acquiesce, whose action pressures the others into doing likewise, is a Jewish woman, described in these terms: 'The first, Rachele Levi, an Israelite, short, very ugly, always full of jewelry, wrote that every day she would give an extra hour of service.'[4]

Rachele Levi bears an identifiably Jewish name. The series of adjectives that follow her naming presumably stem from it and serve to explain it: we learn that she is Jewish, then that she is small and very ugly. The physical description cedes to one that lies halfway between the socially and the physically descriptive: she is 'always full of jewelry.' The wearing of jewelry among the largely impoverished group of telegraph workers would be as inappropriate as it is farfetched. In the story we learn that most of them work because they are constrained to help support their families. A few work to have extra money to spend on themselves. None, however, is described as wealthy enough to be 'always full of jewelry,' which is a step beyond the mere wearing of it. This description presents a major contradiction: the bejeweled appearance of this character is at once offensive to the others, who are poor, and an anomaly in itself, since signs of wealth would make Rachele's having to work an absurdity. She is thus figured as the slyly wealthy Jew who hoards richness and shows it off at the same time. The stereotyping of this character is clear, as is the total marginalization. Even though she is the first to volunteer her service among a rebellious group of co-workers, hers is the least generous of the offers: the others commit themselves to a minimum of several hours per day. Her voluntarism ends up looking like pure opportunism, as it makes her appear willing, whereas the time offered is stingy, once more part of a stereotype. She is guilty of an act of double betrayal: first giving away the solidarity of the group, who had been meeting privately for weeks to organize resistance against this unpaid work, and second offering an amount of time so minimal that it is more token than anything else. Her marginalization is further emphasized by the fact that this is the only mention of her in the story: in the descriptions of the private organizational meetings that took place, her name is never heard.[5]

The first instance of the doubly marginalized woman, Cristina Juliano, serves as a warning as to what is acceptable in terms of difference, especially that which is expressed physically. The second characterization, that of Rachele Levi, can be read as not only a warning but an outright rejection of another kind of difference, an example not only physically unattractive but politically dangerous as well. In 'Telegrafi dello Stato,' Rachele is a threat to society, the figure of the betraying Judas. A seemingly innocent little telegraph worker, she is made to represent a much larger scenario, that of the history of Christian antisemitism. Her gender does not save her, because, as Serao demonstrates in this story, race and religion cut deeper than gender, even deeper than the confusion of gender we see in Cristina.

These characterizations of different kinds of marginality in this early story give some indication of how Serao will later employ the strategy of scapegoating, that is, to preserve a central position for her more mainstream female characters. The politically dangerous side of another marginalized group is more fully developed in her 1913 novel, *La mano tagliata* [The Truncated Hand]. In this text, Serao goes even further in identifying what are essentially social and political problems with bodily ones, as we saw in her love novels discussed in the previous chapter.[6]

The Hand as Clue

In Serao's later fiction, especially after the turn of the century, she became strongly interested in elements of mystery and detection. Novels like *Il delitto di Via Chiatamone* [The Crime of Chiatamone Street] and *La mano tagliata* depend on suspense as a main structural device. Identities are hidden or unknown, orphans abound, criminals lurk in carefully described city streets. The detective model is in fact a particularly appropriate one as we consider the question of marginalization for Serao in her later work.[7]

La mano tagliata demonstrates a conflict between race, religion, and gender that plays out ambivalences and attitudes regarding cultural difference. As we will see, the novel also foregrounds female protagonists at the expense of religious and cultural difference. A reading of the text as it fits into the epistemological framework of mystery fiction will bring out its ideological position as it moves from detective interests into a play of cultural hegemony.[8]

A strong fascination with the material object is one of the distinctive traits of the detective or mystery genre. Dismemberment, death, and displacement of the physical body are not only themes or events that take place in this kind of fiction. These same bodies or body parts can end up speaking for detective epistemologies and ideologies of the texts. Detective epistemology is the combination of the physical and abductive processes by which clues and traces are linked together to solve the mystery at hand.[9]

Both dead bodies and body parts in fiction serve as clues to be read. They lead to the origin of their state; they are traces or residue that have meaning insofar as they point back to what or where they used to be. There are several fundamental differences between the use of an entire dead body and that of dismembered parts. The use of the dead body in fiction is already a complex strategy that generates questions of wholeness and fragmentation; the single separated body part is even more complicated since it evokes a metonymical crisis as well. A dead body motivates a search for the agent of its death, the murderer; a body part requires, instead, a search for the rest of the body as well as for the agent of its fragmentation.

La mano tagliata provides an interesting example of how a body part can be made to speak for larger issues in the text and, moreover, highlight the importance of materiality in the detective or mystery genre. The hand will play several complex roles in this novel. It will speak to a racial or religious confrontation through its functioning as a secular relic and, as a clue leading back to the rest of its body, it will also act an agent of conversion for its protagonist.

The hand in *La mano tagliata* is truncated; it is nonetheless elegant, bejeweled, and feminine. It is found in a lovely velvet case and provides the heuristic direction of the plot. Accidentally left on a train by a mysterious traveler, it is picked up by another traveler, Roberto Alimena, who opens the case, gazes upon the unearthly beauty of the hand, and falls in love with it. The rest of the novel is concerned with Alimena's attempt to locate the original owner of the hand, determine whether she is still alive, and discover the reason for the shocking disfigurement.

The theme of passion is apparent in the novel, but it works in a very different way than in the *drammi di passione,* as Croce called them, that were discussed in the previous chapter. The passion that is highlighted is male passion rather than female. The desire that follows the truncated hand around in the novel and that, indeed, caused its truncation is the passion of two male characters vying for the love of the same woman. The fact that their desire has resulted in the mutilation of a female body is only the beginning of the story.[10]

On first reading, the truncated hand serves primarily as a referent to the rest of the body. Leading and directing the plot in much the same way as the purloined letter of Edgar Allan Poe, the hand does not perform an analogical role, other than that of synecdoche. The traveler who finds the hand falls in love with it because it is part of the whole person – no longer, of course, entirely whole – he longs to meet.

The following is a description of the hand as Roberto Alimena finds it:

> Upon a soft black velvet bed lay a bejeweled feminine hand. Not only the hand, precisely: but also a piece of the arm, cut four inches below the elbow. The hand and piece of arm lay lengthwise in the box: the cover, also made of padded velvet, followed their form and fit together, like a jewel box. . . . [T]he truncated and bejeweled hand was beautiful. Long, with separated tapering fingers, like that of the lover of the divine Raphael, it had perfect lines. It was even placed artistically, with the wrist leaning on the velvet, the palm slightly lifted and the fingertips barely touching, in a light, dignified,

almost immaterial position. The fingernails, pink, shiny, reflected the light from the lamp: they were cut in a half moon
shape: the rim of flesh was pulled away, with elegance. The
hand wasn't pink or white: it was flesh color, a natural
color . . . a hand of a lively color, of a person that was young,
beautiful and healthy: nothing bloodless, waxy, or dark in
that hand . . . so pure of form, of a statuelike appearance, if it
hadn't maintained that telling color of flesh, I would say.[11]

The hand provides a lot of information about its body: the
description makes it clear that this is an upper-class hand,
both by its 'dressing,' as it were, and by its physical condition.
It even speaks for itself: 'quel colore di carne così parlante'
['that telling flesh color']. Isolated as a separate entity from
its body, encased in velvet, covered with jewels, perfect in
color and in line, the hand has become an aesthetic object
whose very materiality is masked, almost overcome, by its
own beauty. Materiality cannot of course be entirely overcome, as is apparent in the way that the hand is 'read' for clues
to its origin. Serao goes to great pains to describe it as 'natural.' I think we may read in this an attempt to normalize the
hand's existence as an entity: to avoid the potential realm of
freakish horror in favor of the world of nonthreatening natural objects.

We learn that this was the hand of one who did not work,
and it shows a 'racial perfection': 'It wasn't fat and round, like
certain pretty and stupid hands: nor thin, like certain hands
that have worked: nor was it a hand that had been often
shaken by other hands, with an aspect of innocence, despite
the luxury of its jewels.'[12]

An essential semiotic question emerges for the reader: How
does a hand, all by itself, as it were, work in a text like this? A
hand usually points somehow or somewhere by means of its
fingers. The image of a hand pointing in a particular direction
is a common semiotic convention.[13] Instead, the truncated
hand points everywhere and nowhere. It points only to itself
as the representation of the rest of the body. It also asks

whether its owner is still alive and, if so, how dead is the severed appendage. How much transference of material status, in this case the status of life or death, can there be between a body and its missing parts?

As we have seen, at first glance the hand looks like a clue: but a hand taken as a clue throws into crisis the usual relationship between clue and crime. Normally, a clue is synecdochically related to a larger object, which is in turn circumstantially or metonymically connected to a solution to the crime, either through a direct relationship to a suspect or to a set of circumstances implicating someone: for example, the cigar ash on the carpet, which belongs to a particular brand of cigar – with any luck an esoteric one! – found only at Shop X, the proprietor of which dimly recalls that the main purchaser of said cigar is a certain mustachioed gentleman who recently moved to town.[14]

To have a body part function as a *clue* is an exaggerated, crude, and parodied instance of this particular, heuristic semiotics. We could argue that it does not function as one at all since a clue typically bears a more complicated relationship to its origin. Umberto Eco's definition of *clue* found in *A Theory of Semiotics* tells us that they are based on complex inferences.[15] It is not a particularly complex inferential move to decide that there must have been a body from which came the hand. The hand is, however, made to function as a clue in the novel since the presence of the hand and absence of the body generate a mystery epistemology. This mystery epistemology structures the text and leads us to the reconnecting of hand and body, which is the solution of the mystery.

Even the apparent complexity of hand-as-clue and its ensuing mystery can be deceptive: the complexity of the hand is not simply limited to its function as a clue. Rather than a simple case of 'pin the tail on the donkey,' or, in this text, the hand on the woman, this object turns out to be much more complicated when seen within the ideological context of the novel.

Reading the Hand

The hand in *La mano tagliata* is an object that both speaks and is read. As a metonym for the rest of its eagerly awaited body, it points to sexual fulfillment vis-à-vis Alimena's desired relationship to the missing body. It also provides a point of convergence, both physical and semiotic, for a dramatic confrontation between different races and religions.

The plot of the novel, while centering around the meandering of the cut-off hand, moves along lines of racial or religious polarization. Most of the major protagonists in the novel are Jewish. They are divided into two groups: the two 'bad' Jewish men, described as dirty, immoral, diabolical, and living in the filth of the ghetto in Rome, and the 'good' Jewish women, who are openly persecuted by the Jewish men.

Mosè Cabib is married to Sara. They have a young daughter, Rachele, who is described in the following manner:

> In Rachele Cabib shone an exalted Jewish feminine beauty. In patriarchal times, her ancestors certainly must have been beautiful, born in the sun of Mesopotamia, wandering through the flowering valleys and stopping at cool fountains: so must have been Rebecca, the noble girl: so must have been Herodias, she who fatally took the head of John the Baptist from Tetrarch. Rachele was tall and slender and in her form there was infinite grace and seduction: her every movement had a harmonic sense which completed the purity of her lines. She was pale and a little dark complected, but the dark of ivory, warm and vivid, an admirable complexion, where the blood of youth and of health ran together, both vigorous and fine. Very black was her hair and her eyes a deep black, shaped like almonds, half closed under ivory brows and long curved eyelashes. In her eyes there was a mysterious thoughtful expression, an impenetrable secret that aroused an unsatisfied curiosity. Her face was oval, in a soft and caressing line, her mouth was red and tumid, a little proud, not given to smiles and words. Beautiful![16]

This description of Rachele is particularly interesting for two reasons. First, it presents her from the point of view of a male spectator, remarking enthusiastically on her beauty and seductive powers and containing eroticized descriptions such as 'her mouth was red and tumid.' Second, it takes place against the backdrop of biblical imagery, and it is precisely this landscape that makes this benevolent description possible. In this imagery, the problematic split between Judaism and Christianity has not yet occurred; biblical Jews as the forerunners of Christianity have typically been described in this positive light throughout the history of the Christian representation of Jews. The female characters in the novel are identified with this Old Testament model of the Jew. The male characters, on the other hand, are made to represent modernity and all its ensuing problems. Since they refuse to convert in the text, they also represent what might ironically be called Judaism after the Fall: the refusal of Jews to accept Jesus and become Christians.

The association of male Jews with the ills of modernity is particularly clear in the case of the main male protagonist in the novel, Marcus Henner. An 'evil' Jewish doctor by trade, Henner sees Sara one day in a Moscow synagogue and falls desperately in love with her. In order to get closer to her, he befriends her husband Mosè and involves him in various schemes, attempting to convince Mosè that he could divine the secrets of the world (including the location of buried treasure) by hypnotizing Sara. However, when Henner does so, she falls into a dangerous coma. He takes her away with him, assuring Mosè that she will die otherwise.

Henner cuts off her hand without anaesthesia in order to shock her out of the coma. He then keeps her prisoner for fifteen years, hoping that she will eventually return his love. These events have already occurred at the outset of the narrative, but the reader learns about them only in Henner's confession at the end of the text.

Fifteen years later, Henner has developed a passion for the

now-grown-up Rachele, who strongly resembles her mother both in her looks and in her aversion to him. He begins insisting that Rachele marry him. Rachele's father, Mosè, is most interestingly named, as this rendition of Moses is not one that could save his people: on the contrary, he is ready to betray his daughter by delivering her into the hands of Henner. Rather than save his wife, he has already allowed her to be taken away and kept by Henner for fifteen years. In a reenactment of the abduction of his wife, he attempts to deliver his daughter directly to her persecutor. The rewriting of the biblical Moses through the actions of Mosè is indisputably dark and points up the contrast between the female and male Jewish characters. Another peculiar aspect of the name Mosè is that Henner himself aspires to be the most important and powerful Jew besides Moses, describing himself in his confession as 'the man who stole from God the secret of dominating human willpower, the most glorious son of Israel after Moses.'[17]

Naming plays a significant role in this novel: in fact, it indicates the characters' religious status. Sara, Mosè's wife, converts to Catholicism and takes the name of Maria. Sarah is a prominent figure in the cast of biblical ancestors in the Jewish tradition. She and her husband Abraham were the first Jews; she is thus the first Jewish woman and the first Jewish mother, giving birth to Isaac at the advanced age of ninety or so.[18] Sara's renaming as Maria is more than just coincidental, as it indicates not only a conversion from one religion to another – conversion to Catholicism certainly does not require a change of name – but a symbolic passage as well from the first Jewish woman to the first Christian female figure.[19]

Rachele falls in love with a Christian aristocrat named Ranieri Lambertini, who wants to rescue her from the sad, dark, and dirty ghetto (and by implication away from her Jewish life, which takes on the same connotations as its physical surroundings). Henner discovers the plan and arranges an ambush of Lambertini, who is wounded but recovers and goes off in search of Rachele. To avoid Henner's persecution,

Rachele has converted to Catholicism and sought refuge in a convent called '*Le sepolte vive*' [The Buried Alive]. Roberto continues to follow the traces of the truncated hand, which bring him to London. In the meantime, his scientist friend, Silvio Amati, has researched the interesting new embalming method used to preserve the hand and discovered that the only scientist who could have performed such advanced and ingenious work was indeed Marcus Henner. Thus the two threads of the plot, one concerned with Rachele and Ranieri and the other with Maria and Roberto, definitively come together through the empirical and scientific evidence that the persecutor of both Roberto and Ranieri is the same person.

Roberto manages to steal Maria away from Henner's London house, and the two flee and spend a blissful month together on an island. Henner finds out where they are and spends two days on a boat near their villa attempting to hypnotize Maria from afar to make her leap to her death from a balcony. He succeeds, then repents of his vile persecution and murder of this woman, leaves a long confession on her grave, and rather heroically kills himself. This confession, along with a long letter from Maria to her daughter instructing her to leave the convent and marry Lambertini, are taken to Lambertini in Rome.

Henner, the plot's focal character, has a most telling genealogical background. His father was a doctor and his mother a cultivator of magic. Having learned from both, Henner merges the two disciplines in his interest in hypnotism and parapsychology. Overcoming even the stigma of his 'foul Semitic origin' ['turpe origine semita'], he becomes known throughout Europe for his exceptional ability to cure difficult medical cases through hypnotism. His second major contribution to the scientific world is the preservation of human flesh through a new embalming fluid he has developed and perfected.

Henner suffers from megalomania as a result of his scientific genius, which leads him to describe himself as Messiah.

Called 'The Master' ['Il Maestro'] by his followers, he has a split personality, leaning both toward the figure of a martyr and toward a religiously inspired evil. Acting as a leader in the international Jewish community, Jews come to visit him from all over Europe at night to make plans for unknown purposes and ends, a secret he keeps hidden from the Christian authorities. We learn in Henner's confession that this clandestine political activity is concerned with philanthropic efforts to raise money to help Jewish communities: 'That sovereignty that the people of Israel no longer possess, I could have restored to them, with my power and the help of the great Jewish millionaires. I could have put myself at the head of my people!'[20]

Once again, this passage produces a mixed effect. Point of view is crucial in this text, as illustrated here. Henner's activities – in particular his nocturnal meetings with other disenfranchised Jews – can seem benign, even philanthropic, or conspiratorial, again a stereotype. Henner's goal of restoring dignity to the Jewish people can in fact be seen as noble, until it is combined with his megalomaniacal ambition and with the stereotype of 'great Jewish millionaires.' Much of the tension in this text is created by the discrepancies between various points of view about cultural and religious differences.

The Jew as Other

Serao's attitude toward Jews and Judaism in this novel can be contextualized from a reading of some of her essays about a trip to Palestine in 1893. The essays were later collected and published in 1899 as *Nel paese di Gesù: Ricordi di un viaggio in Palestina* [In the Land of Jesus: Memoirs of a Trip to Palestine], a work describing her reaction to what she saw in Palestine and religious, spiritual, and political interpretations of her impressions. Her description of the inhabitants of Jerusalem reveals even more than what she saw:

But among the sixty thousand people who reside within its sacred walls, is there, perhaps, a people of Jerusalem? Who would then merit this elect name, envied among others and dear to the Lord? Not the Jews who make up, at this point, half, over half, of the inhabitants of Jerusalem. Israel had had an immeasurable gift, a divine promise, had had the sublime reality of the greatest future that has ever been reserved for a people: but she got tired of being pious, good, happy. From that fatal Thursday of the month of Nissam on which the Jews, strangely angry and blind with fury against the Nazarone, insisted, they insisted, that the blood of that Just Man fall on their heads and on the heads of their children, the called-for malediction struck them and they were dispersed, they were no longer a nation, no longer a people. . . . [T]he Jews have begun to return to Jerusalem. They are returning there from all the countries of Europe, pallid, tired, almost always sickly, with the timid air of beaten dogs, glancing obliquely at everyone, fearing in everyone an enemy, a persecutor, taciturn, thoughtful, incapable of arguing. . . . [T]hey distinguish themselves above all by a constant air of weakness, of illness, even in the young people and children.[21]

Serao's arguments range from conventional Catholic antisemitism picturing Jews as Christ-killers to a kind of sociological antipathy masked as piety in her description of the physical condition of these recent immigrants from Europe. She goes beyond even conventional antisemitism in her rhetorical structures, emphasizing the Jews' purported desire to kill Jesus ('vollero, essi vollero' ['they insisted, they insisted']) and describing their expulsion from the Holy Land as self-generated and masochistic. The image of the Jew as sick and weak belongs to the repertoire of antisemitic discourse.[22]

The language of this passage reminds us of *La mano tagliato*. The dark side to Henner's personality, for example, is portrayed both physically and ideologically.[23] Henner is described as a monstrous figure:

The Master was seated in Mosè Cabib's old armchair and his small, deformed and stiff body was lost in that wide chair.

He kept his hands on the black leather armrests and in the shadow they seemed white and rigid like those of a monster. Despite the lack of light, one saw a truly horrible face, more than pallid, it was dissipated, with protruding cheekbones and a prominent jaw; a hairless upper lip and a few grizzled and unkempt hairs on his cheeks; a mouth cut in a straight line, like a sharp wound, with thin lips, rosy bordering on crimson; a mouth full of large yellow teeth; a receding forehead, from which sprouted a strange head of hair, almost red, but these too fine and unkempt, thus tangled like undergrowth. And finally those green, green, green eyes, like green water, glacial, sometimes flashing, sometimes simply glassy. The body was deformed: a hump on the left shoulder twisted that enormous torso on those short, thin, ignoble legs. He was horrible.[24]

Henner is stigmatized in three ways here: as Jew, hunchback, and evil scientist. His family is not Italian, but is described as Austrian, and is transient at that, having moved frequently from Germany to Russia to Italy and England. The Jews who appear in the novel are never indigenous; they are always migratory, the stereotype of the wandering Jew: in fact, this is the same stereotype presented by Serao in her essay on Jerusalem.

Henner has his own agenda that is inextricably linked to the politics of religious and cultural confrontation in the text. His goal of persecuting Christians is laid out in his confession, as he says: 'But especially upon Christians I practiced all my abilities as hypnotist and all the magic secrets from my mother. Ah, how I hated these Christians and how I destroyed them, all those who happened under my power! How I broke their hearts and ruined their existence, without their being able to understand my vendetta!'[25]

There is yet another reversal in this text: the strange persecution fantasy of Christians by Jews. Henner explains, 'It was an old vendetta, the one I practiced against them, even though I was at heart a pious man and loved the God of Abraham and Moses; it was a vendetta for our fallen Temple, for our cast-down faith, our dispersed nation, our destroyed fortune: the vendetta against the Christians, against these wild beasts who appeared mild who have persecuted us for centuries, who don't give us respite and who are now in our hands, because we are the richest, the more clever, the strongest, and the more audacious.'[26]

Described by Mosè as the 'Lord of Death,' Henner's powers are seen as rivaling those of God, as he uses his scientific abilities and an understanding of the occult to hypnotize and to heal. The unethical nature of his practice is called into question on two counts. First, we learn in his confession that he often used hypnosis to take advantage of women sexually while they were in a trance. The only character whom Henner was unable to hypnotize to this level was Maria. Second, we are informed that most of his 'healing' involved convincing patients under hypnosis, even those suffering from serious disease, that they were well.

Henner is established as a rival to the 'true' maestro of the text, the figure of Jesus to whom the converts turn in their desperation. The combination of Henner's powers and his agenda regarding Christians make the figure of Henner a kind of Antichrist-like character. He and Mosè frequently make anti-Christian remarks, which further marginalize them from the Christian culture in which they live. Identifying them as clear threats to Serao's primarily Christian readership accentuates the various negative stereotypes she has already presented and reinforces the stereotype of the Jewish conspiracy. Rachele flees from Henner and finally recounts her tale to the abbess of *Le sepolte vive,* who responds in shock, 'An implacable persecution!' Cabib, when he discovers that his daughter has been secretly reading Manzoni's *I promessi sposi* [The Betrothed], calls it 'one of those nasty bad books by these Christians.'[27] In his doubly sanctified position as both the author of the great novel of the nineteenth century and a famous convert to Catholicism, Manzoni furnishes an absolutely inflammatory target of attack.

Serao's use of certain ideological constructs in this novel is highlighted by the fact that all three Jewish women have converted to Catholicism and changed their names in the process. The name changing represents the larger change in identity of these protagonists. Conversion from one religion to another is not the only issue at stake here. The renaming is also a symbolic change of race. Old Testament names become New Testament ones: Sara becomes Maria, Rachele becomes Grazia, and Clara, Henner's wife, also becomes Maria. The scenario of all Jewish women converting from a religion conferred by matrilineal descent creates a discourse of symbolic genocide.

The question of racism, and, moreover, the relation of race to religion, is posed by this text. The female characters are depicted as belonging to another race than the male characters. The hand itself, which we later learn belongs to Maria, is described as being racially pure and becomes a fetishistic object for one of the Christian protagonists. Once again, a reading of the hand provides some answers to these questions.

The Hand as Relic

The hand, an object situated squarely in the middle of this religious and racial confrontation, can be analyzed from another vantage point as well, its value as a relic. A body part separated from the rest of its text, the body, and singled out for special attention brings to mind the Christian strategy by which a fragment or bodily remains are invested with meaning. Considering the hand as a relic illuminates the way in which the text's ideologies are incorporated and clarified.

A relic is a fragment pertaining in some way to the historical physical presence of a holy body or an object that came into contact with a holy body. Like the embalmed hand, it comprises incorruptible remains. It can be an actual piece of the body, such as a saint's finger, or can reflect more distant degrees of contiguity, such as a piece of the shroud used to wrap the body or a piece of the fabric used to wrap the cross that held the holy body. As the historian P. R. L. Brown reminds us, the medieval world was full of significant tombs and relics.[28] According to Brown, 'relics needed status. . . . [A] relic that is not acclaimed is, candidly, not a relic.' Relics whose status was uncertain were 'caught in a spiral of ambiguity.'[29] The strategies of what makes a relic a relic are interesting and pertain to our case of a hand. Of fundamental importance are recognition and belief: in other words, a dependency on human practice.

Looking at the hand as a secular relic in this novel raises some comments and questions. First, it points out the absence of the holy. The very way in which the hand posits itself as secular relic emphasizes the absence of a holy body. Second, it also emphasizes the banality of the Catholicism represented in the novel, which is reduced to its simplest elements and then subverted by this unholy relic.

One might question how the hand can be considered a relic at all if it is not part of a religiously significant body or object. The answer lies in what a relic can and must do. It both stands for and embodies a power and belief beyond itself. Its efficacy as a relic is based on a relation between power and belief; the participant believes that the relic has power, and the relic is supposed to bring one something or do something for one.

In this novel the hand becomes a relic specifically because of its relationship to Roberto Alimena, who faithfully believes that it represents some kind of miracle, that it is a living part of a still-living female body. He is unswayed despite his scientist friend's testimony that no one could have survived the truncation: 'He alone, tenaciously, had believed with an unshakeable faith that that hand was from a still-living person.'[30] The encounter with the hand has effected a kind of conversion for Alimena: described as an apathetic aristocrat, he has changed, as he says himself in a letter to Maria: 'If you knew what a dry, perverse, cold, hateful person I was! If you saw what a tender, pious, mystic, devoted, pure soul I have now, because I love you, because your dear hand came under my lips!'[31] This conversion, although motivated by love, carries strong religious implications: Alimena's soul has become pious, devoted, and pure as a result of his exposure to Maria's hand.

The hand has power for him because he believes in its strange immortality and because it eventually leads him to her. The power that the hand embodies is of course secular, since it both represents and acts out the power of semiotics, of a trace to lead to and reconstitute meaning. The unit of meaning in this case is the re-membered and, more important, reconstituted female figure. Alimena recognizes the hand as a relic and believes in its power to lead him to the woman. As we will see, it is the very question and kind of reconstitution that is crucial to the ideological structure of the text.

Brown, in the article cited above, discusses the medieval notion of *reverentia,* as he says, 'a focussing of belief onto precise, if invisible objects in such a way as to lay the participants under specific obligations.'[32] There is as well a relationship between the episodes in a participant's life and his or her 'good and bad relations with this specific, if invisible, object.'[33] Here of course the object or relic is not invisible, nor did it have to be in medieval times, but the point remains the same. The hand was not a relic for Henner: not only did he not believe in it as such – he saw it rather as a painful reminder of an insane act of cruelty on his part – but also he did not have what Brown would call a 'good relation' to it. Therefore, the hand passes to Alimena, who will revere and esteem it. This moment of internal textual logic dictates the terms on which the hand is considered. Alimena's relation to the hand is good, and it obediently leads him to what he desires.

The fact that Maria does not ultimately survive the transformation of a part of her body into a relic adds an interesting twist to this secular tale. First the hand gains status as a relic, since a relic is not supposed to come from a body still living. Second, it underlines the conditions of her life and death. She dies a modified version of the virgin martyr: after fifteen years of separation from her daughter and protecting her chastity from the evil scientist, she is murdered in an act that mimics and degrades a divine power. Henner's ability to overcome her will from a distance and force her into self-annihilation surprises even the megalomaniac himself and causes his downfall as well.

The hand does not function primarily as a symbol: it is first and foremost a physical point of convergence for these issues, whose meaning depends on and is generated by the material status of the hand. It is the physical act of truncation and subsequent geographical separation from the body that invests the hand with meaning. The system of signification remains stubbornly self-referential. This use of a part of the body is an insistently literal one, in which the materiality of the object is much more important than any figurative or symbolic value it might have; in fact, it avoids such a reading. The figuring of the hand moves beyond an immediate materiality to what we could call a physical reading of the symbolic: that is, as relic.

In the appearance of the convent called *Le sepolte vive*, Christianity as a solution to the characters' problems is taken to an extreme. This convent, described as a refuge for women from the tribulations of the world, is in essence a complete escape from a hostile society. Once inside, nuns do not ever have to see a person from the outside world again. If they do desire such contact, they are permitted to speak to visitors, who are allowed only once a year, through a thick wall. The convent is even a tomb, as the text explains to us that the nuns were buried at death inside the convent walls until the city of Naples forbade the practice. The nature of the convent and also its name suggest textual irony regarding Catholicism as a solution to the problems of women in society. It is likely that *Le sepolte vive* was actually a Neapolitan nickname for cloistered nuns. In this text, however, the idea of cloistering, by no means an unusual practice for certain orders, is manipulated. *Le sepolte vive* is not taken seriously as a solution to the problem of women's place in the world; it is instead a melodramatic staging of the plight of Rachele, called 'Suora Grazia' inside its walls and described as 'the poor Jewess who became Christian,' until Ranieri can rescue her from being 'buried alive.' This text, like the others discussed in the preceding chapter, preserves the interests of 'love,' which cannot be served by leaving the young, beautiful female protagonist to such a fate.

Christianity, more specifically Catholicism, in the novel is tied to conversion, salvation, and hope. Judaism in the novel is presented as grossly material and scientific, epitomized in this strange truncation by a Jewish doctor who himself seems to stand for evil incarnate and the Antichrist. The Jewish ideology is prejudicially portrayed, while the Catholic one is simplistic. What is not simplistic in this text is the relation between the two, played out by the hand, and the role that medical science plays in the novel to further the confrontation between the two 'races' and religion itself. The way in which the interplay between Catholic and Jewish religious structures works in this text is similar to Lombroso's analysis of tefillin, discussed in chapter 3. Here too it is the logic of one religion that is adopted in order to provide a skewed 'reading' of the other.

Conclusion: Race, Religion, and Gender

Science and religious ideology are inextricably intertwined in *La mano tagliata*, just as passion and illness are inseparable in *Addio amore!* The image of science presented is highly ambivalent, all the more complicated by the religious politics that are embedded within this image. Marcus Henner, it is to be remembered, is the son of a witch and a medical doctor. His 'science' of hypnosis is new and controversial; his methods, particularly that of dismemberment, both highly dramatic and inhumane. Is Henner portrayed as a scientist because he is Jewish, or is it the other way around? In other words, to what degree is his own marginalization in the text attributable to his *method* or to his *culture*? And to what

point is the text attempting to obfuscate the differences between the two? Is what we might call the politics of cultural
cross-hybridism, the seemingly ungodly marriage of witch-
craft and medicine, made possible because this wedding can
take place on the cultural and religious fringes? It would appear at first reading that the nature of science and its discourse
of power are so ultimately corrupting that the religious discourse cannot be separated from the scientific one. A chapter
from the history of antisemitism, will, however, furnish a different perspective on the situation.

Jewish physicians from the Renaissance on had been viewed
as both healers and poisoners of Christians, as Gilman recounts.[34] In explaining the origins of this stereotype, Gilman gives the example of Johannes Pfefferkorn, a convert
from Judaism to Catholicism who began writing antisemitic
pamphlets under the direction of the Cologne Dominicans in
1507. As Gilman says of one of these pamphlets and its relation to a developing discourse about Jews and language,

> After condemning the usurers, he [Pfefferkorn] warns that
> the Jewish doctors are quacks who use the practice of medi-
> cine to poison Christians. The function and status of the
> medical profession is not being drawn into question. It is
> only the Jewish doctor that Pfefferkorn is attacking. The
> association of the hidden language of the Jews, not as white
> magic but as black magic, with treating the ill parallels the
> beginning of systematic persecution of witches in northern
> Europe. The fear that that which can cure can also kill is
> associated with the view that the healer has powers from
> some supernatural force, a force that is most probably ma-
> levolent.[35]

The notion of black magic as that which underlies the science of the Jewish physician is quite clearly not an original
idea in Serao. Her portrait of Henner is complicated by the
genealogical and ideological frame in which we find him.
Serao underlines the questionable nature of his science by
problematizing the role of his parents in his very creation as

the Messiah-genius–evil doctor. Note that the evil Jewish physician of antisemitic tradition is always a *male* figure. Serao intensifies and complicates her argument by also marshaling an evil maternal figure, the mother-as-witch.

Here, too, a binary opposition is present in the figure of the 'good' scientist, Silvio Amati. He is portrayed as a well-known scientist who teaches at the university, has a laboratory and assistants, and clearly works within the bounds of acceptable scientific behavior. Amati is even described as physically resembling Charles Darwin. His science is ideologically under control, unlike that of Marcus Henner. As an 'impartial' scientist, he is able to show great admiration and respect for the genius of Marcus Henner without entering into the ideological debates over Henner's social and religious unacceptability in which the other characters engage. The apparent dangers of out-of-control science are thus tempered in Serao's presentation of the 'good' scientist, who is not a threat to society.

The religious politics in *La mano tagliata* are bound up with gender politics as well. The question of the Jew as marginalized brings us to the suspiciously absent issue of marginalized woman in the novel. The Jew occupies the liminal territory of the outsider, as we can see by the descriptions of and roles played by the Jewish male characters. Yet some of the Jewish characters are female, and they are not liminal at all. The potential marginality of these characters is passed over by the problem of the Jew, thereby allowing the female characters who convert to remain central figures. In other words, the notion of the Jew as marginalized substitutes for woman as such. This at least appears to be the case on a first reading. More detailed analysis of the situation, however, provides another viewpoint.

Judaism and Christianity are paired as incompatible opposites, one of which must take on the position of the other, just as female and male characters form binary oppositions. Judaism is put in the position of ceding to Christianity, just as the Jewish women in the text convert to Christianity in order to move ahead, away from Jewish men and away as well from a culture and religion presented as atavistic. This is a twisted Weiningerian scenario presented in a fictive form: the identification of the male Jew with femininity in Weininger's text becomes here the aligning of male Jew with Judaism and female Jews with Catholicism – published at approximately the same time as Weininger's *Sex and Character* in Italian. Once again, antisemitic discourse becomes mixed up with gender issues, as we have seen in the cases of both Lombroso and Weininger.

The recoupable position in Serao's text, the centralized role that avoids the stigma of marginality, is preserved not so much for the woman but for Catholicism itself. To what degree does this text attempt to preserve a culturally dominant position for Catholicism and to what degree is the figure of the woman merely an *agent* to that end?

What then is at stake in the cultural, religious, and racial confrontation in this novel? The text provides a clear agenda. First is the attempt to construct one religious and racial configuration and substitute it for another, that is to say, conversion: not in its usual sense of leaving one religion for another but in a much more extreme way. Not only does the soul repent and the penitent embrace a new and different religious structure, but furthermore a physical transfer of religious or mythic construct occurs. Maria loses her hand to a diabolical doctor of her own 'race'; the hand is then found by a Christian who recognizes it for what it is, a Christian object of worship – albeit in a secular context – and he is subsequently transformed in the encounter with the 'holy' hand. The events set in motion by the truncation lead to Maria's most Christian death. The conversion is not achieved by a change *in* the God or *of* the God to whom she prays, but by what happens to her flesh, both before and after death.

Even if we take conversion to mean simply a change of religion, the term is still problematic in a text that so strongly emphasizes the racial differences between two religious groups.

Conversion from one race to another is simply impossible. The ultimate difficulty in conversion in the text involves once again the hand. Conversion to Catholicism does not usually require a change of flesh on the part of the acolyte. In this text, however, Maria must lose her hand in order to achieve first a conversion rendered problematic by race and then a Christian death. Her death signals the impossibility of a simple conversion from one race to another, which brings into play complex issues regarding the precise identity of race and religion.

Point of view is paramount in this text and is in fact the source of some of the complexity of the religious and gender politics. The status of the two female protagonists, Maria and her daughter Rachele, is established in an interesting and complicated way. They are seen by the male characters primarily in terms of their desirability. The narrative point of view more often expresses the male characters' desires for these women than the perspective of the women themselves. This aspect is particularly clear in the eroticized description of Rachele quoted earlier.

The problem of perspective extends even further. The inappropriateness or even impossibility of Jews having sexual relations with Christians comes up often in the text, from both Jewish and Christian characters: 'A Jewish woman cannot be either the lover or the wife of a Christian,' Mosè tells his daughter when he discovers she's in love with Ranieri. Henner writes in his confession, 'A Jewish woman can be unfaithful to her husband, but never with a man of another religion.' Similar words come from Roberto Alimena in a conversation with detective Dick Leslie as they try to determine Maria's relationship to Marcus Henner. When Roberto hears that Maria is Christian, he says, 'So she's not his wife!' Leslie answers, 'Lover perhaps . . .' and Roberto responds, 'Isn't that impossible, with a Jew?'[36] He is not entirely sure if this 'impossibility' is a legal or a moral one. Several questions arise from the situating of what is essentially the Jewish sexuality of Rachele against the backdrop of male Christian desire. We are left wondering whether the primary reason for Maria's and Rachele's conversion is to make them sexually available to Ranieri and Roberto. The seemingly threatening relationship of 'Jewish sexuality' to Christian desire in this text ultimately raises the question of what it means to polarize sexuality not simply along lines of gender but along religious lines as well. An odd aspect to these issues is that historically the text is set just after the turn of the century, when the ghettos of Italy were no longer closed. In 1913 there were no legal restrictions to the intermarrying of Christians and Jews, nor would there be until the racial laws of 1938. The text straddles two historical periods in which similar restrictions did exist: one before the setting of the text, and one, eerily enough, twenty-five years later.

The use of Jewish characters in the novel and the cultural and religious issues it generates is a way of masking another agenda on Serao's part: that of critiquing the patriarchy. Once again the margins are moved: instead of making male Christian characters reprehensible for their actions, 'evil,' as it were, she transfers her criticism onto the figure of the male Jew. This particular reading of Serao's agenda does not detract from the antisemitism in the text: rather, it reinforces it, as it becomes clear that only through a negatively viewed scapegoat is this critique of patriarchy possible.

The problematics of conversion and the confusion of gender and religious politics in *La mano tagliata* generate the elusive and shifting nature of marginalization, an issue which is also apparent in 'Telegrafi dello stato.' If the attempted conversion of the female protagonists from Jewish to Christian cannot work because of the overwhelming materiality of the hand, then Serao's denial of the role of the marginalized – here woman – cannot work either. The attempt to displace the identity of the gendered and racial figure of the other is seen to fail in these terms. It is in part the insistence on material constructs in this text that sabotages the ultimately impossible dual project of changing the identity of marginalization and of recentering woman in Serao's fictive world.

CHAPTER SEVEN

GENDER & THE STIGMA OF DIFFERENCE

The history of the use of the word *stigma,* the singular of *stigmata,* illuminates our understanding of the physical and cultural vilification of difference apparent in both Lombroso and Serao and so central to the late nineteenth-century scientific and cultural landscape. Stigma can in fact be read as a figure for difference, and a consideration of the usages and meanings of the word brings together the issues of Judaism and gender raised in the works of Lombroso and Serao.

According to the *Oxford English Dictionary* (OED), *stigma* is bestowed with the following meanings:

1. A mark made upon the skin by burning with a hot iron . . . as a token of infamy or subjection; a brand.

2. fig, a mark of disgrace or infamy; a sign of severe censure or condemnation.

3. marks resembling the wounds on the crucified body of Christ, said to have been supernaturally impressed on the bodies of certain saints and other devout persons.

4. Path. a morbid spot, dot, or point on the skin, esp. one which bleeds spontaneously.[1]

The primary meaning of *stigma* is quite literally a branding, a bodily mark that distinguishes the individual as someone who is vilified, presumably through unacceptable behavior, class status, and so on. The stigmatized one is thus isolated through this physical marking on the body. The first meaning shows how the figurative denotation of the verb *to stigmatize,* hinted at in the second definition above, would have developed.

The OED gives textual examples of the words it defines, both to show them in context and to recreate the historical panorama in which the words have developed and functioned. The illustration given for the first meaning of *stigma* is the following: '1596, Harington, Meta. "circumcision . . . impressing a painful stigma, or caracter in God's peculiar people."' This particular use of stigma is striking for a number of reasons. First, it defines circumcision more than it defines stigma. 'God's peculiar people' is an obvious reference to the Jews. The definition of stigma in this context delineates circumcision as well, as we learn that, for this author, circumcision is a 'painful' stigma, belonging to a people defined by the word 'peculiar.' Thus, stigma is a mark of both difference and peculiarity. Moreover, if it were not for this peculiarity, there would be no marking, no vilification, no painful difference. The fact that this is a self-chosen marking is merely part of the peculiarity.

The first three meanings of stigma have some bearing on what constitutes the logic of difference for Lombroso. *Stigmata* is the term used by Lombroso to refer to signs of the born criminal. Although he is not the originator of medical use of the word, his wholehearted adoption and frequent usage of a term imbued with strong Christian connotations seem problematic for a Jewish scientist, as I noted in chapter 2.[2] But this is not the end of the stigma story for Lombroso. The second meaning is relevant to Lombroso's project as well, for the way in which he categorizes the born criminal marks the individual in more than just a physical sense. It is clear from reading Lombroso that his method creates a cultural and social parenthesis for this socially undesirable group. The ability to recognize the physical signs of born criminals, whether or not they are practicing their 'innate' trade, implies their marginalization as well and an attempt to control their difference.

The third meaning of stigma, referring to Jesus' wounds caused by the nails on the cross and the spear, relates to Lombroso as well. In a predominantly Christian culture, this meaning is permanently imbedded in the other meanings, even though it is not listed as the primary one. The wounds of Jesus as a metaphor for the suffering of humankind might seem at first glance contrary to Lombroso's use of stigmata as that which distinguishes the criminal as an atavistic throwback and a threat to society. According to Christian theology, however, it is no accident that the wounds of Jesus came to be called stigmata, referring to criminal wounds of infamy, for in this theology there is an insistence that Jesus was treated like a criminal by the Roman authorities. Thus the wounds of criminal infamy become a badge of honor and a symbol for martyrdom, forever changing the implications of the word *stigmata* in the process.

The religious significance of stigmata still seems to present some difficulties for Lombroso. He uses the word *piaghe,* wounds, to describe the wounds of modernity which the Jews bear, yet the word can also refer to the wounds of Jesus. Describing the wounds of modernity through the metaphor of stigmata would seem to present an oxymoron: that which is too modern is actually too atavistic as well. Lombroso's complicated view of stigmata and the dangers of using a Christian metaphor to describe the Jews become clear: if he believes that stigmata refer to signs of atavism, what does that say about his view of the wounds of Jesus?

The fourth definition of stigma, spontaneous bleeding from the skin, sheds even more light on the interstice between cultural difference and its physical representation. In this sense of the word, the religious significance of stigmata intersects with the medical, as saints and other holy persons were believed to bleed spontaneously from the skin as imitations of the stigmata of Jesus, thereby showing their holiness and faith. Serao's *Addio amore!,* discussed in chapter 4, explores this strange and rather wonderful collision between a banal bleeding for a lost lover, a bleeding that is simultaneously a sign of hysteria and a sign of faith and martyrdom to the 'love' that both Serao and Lombroso theorize as a kind of slavery for women.

The second definition of stigma gives rise to the notion of *stigmatization,* the idea that an individual or group is permanently tainted in society's imagination and it refers to the social and cultural consequences of difference. This marking is not necessarily visible to the naked eye but is indelible all the same and serves to distinguish or set the group apart. For Lombroso, the moment of reckoning comes when circumcision, that 'painful stigma,' becomes his own physical and indelible mark. The correlation made by the sixteenth-century author cited in the OED between circumcision and stigmatization that is clearly as much cultural as it is physical is at the heart of Lombroso's own assessments of circumcision. Outlined in chapter 3, Lombroso's analyses of the practice of circumcision for the Jews ranges from a 'leftover of cannibalism' to a 'cruel practice performed with stone knives and the teeth.' The connections between the Lombrosian figuring of circumcision as a painful and peculiar stigma and a vampiristic scenario are close indeed and are strengthened by Lombroso's attitudes toward bleeding in general and menstruation in particular. Lombroso's view of the stigma of menstruation runs parallel to that of circumcision: both are gendered signs of difference with specific meanings within Judaism.

What this scenario points to is, once again, the cultural stigmatization that accompanies the physical mark. And it is clearly the cultural stigmatization that most concerns Lombroso, as my analysis of his attitudes toward Jewish religious practices demonstrates. The more visible the practice, the more Lombroso condemns it. The more the Jews appear outwardly different from their neighbors, the more he attacks the practices that create the atmosphere of difference. Neither Lombroso nor Weininger attacks the Jews for theological differences from Christianity per se, nor do they attempt to demonstrate that the 'real' problem with the Jews is their refusal to accept Christ, the more common attack from Christian sources throughout the history of antisemitism. Seen in this light, the critique of both Lombroso and Weininger can be seen as a specifically Jewish one, intimately connected to the uncomfortableness of difference for them.

For Serao, the stigmata of difference are gendered, as she attempts to escape the imprisonment of her sex. She endeavors to free her female protagonists from this fate while simultaneously admitting the impossibility of doing so in a patriarchal society. Stigmata as a term of difference connected to both what is Jewish, the mark of circumcision, and what is most radically not Jewish, the stigmata of Jesus, point to a gender crisis as well. It is the male Jew who bears the brunt of Lombroso's critique of circumcision, yet in Lombroso's landscape of the virile prostitute, the sexually ill female Jew, and the male Jew who ultimately pays for the sexual sins of the female, circumcision becomes emblematic as well of the gendered status of the stigmatized Jew. In his inability to distance himself from his subject, all Jews are ultimately male for Lombroso, even though he singles out female Jews for a specialized and sexualized attack. And all Jews figure as female for Weininger, who feminizes the Jew into a single sex. For Serao, the figure of the Jew is predominantly male, as she converts her female Jewish characters in order to save them both from patriarchy and from marginality. The convergence of what is Jewish and what is gender becomes a drama in itself, as the definitions and particular stigma of various kinds of cultural difference merge in the eyes of these theorists.

NOTES

Chapter 1: The Taint of the Quagga

1. Charles Darwin, *The Variation of Plants and Animals Under Domestication*, 435.

2. Ibid., 428.

3. Richard W. Burkhardt, 'Closing the Door on Lord Morton's Mare: The Rise and Fall of Telegony,' 2.

4. This experiment began in 1984 when scientists at the University of California, Berkeley, were able to extract DNA from the skin of a quagga held by a German museum. Through DNA comparison, they determined that the quagga was a closer relative to the zebra than to the horse. See *The New York Times*, May 11, 1993, C10.

5. Steven Jay Gould, in *Hen's Teeth and Horse's Toes*, 376–80, discusses how the stripes that were purportedly from the quagga's influence were in fact the result of a regressive trait that would cause them eventually to appear in the breeding of horses. He cites J. C. Ewart's 1896 breeding experiments, which demonstrated the appearance of these stripes in horses, thereby disproving the quagga's role in relation to the stripes found on the foals sired by the Arabian stallion. This experiment does not, however, address the question of the foals' manes, which also resembled those of the quagga.

6. See, e.g., Cynthia Eagle Russett, *Sexual Science: The Construction of Victorian Womanhood*, for a discussion of variability and the way it was used to argue the inferiority of women and certain racial groups.

7. Gillian Beer, *Darwin's Plots: Evolutionary Narrative in Darwin, George Eliot and Nineteenth-Century Fiction*, 17.

8. The terms *racialist* and *racist* and their definitions have been a source of debate among scholars involved in studying racism and

its development. For discussions of this problem, see Henry Louis Gates, ed. *'Race,' Writing, and Difference.*

9. For more on the liberal politics of Darwin, see Stephen Jay Gould, 'In Praise of Charles Darwin,' 1–4.

10. Reproduced in Karl Pearson, *The Life, Letters and Labours of Francis Galton,* 159.

11. Alberto Cavaglion, 'Svevo and Weininger (Lord Morton's Horse).'

12. 'Chi sa che il figlio di Filippo Arborio non sia, come si dice, *tutto il mio ritratto.* L'accomodamento allora sarà anche più facile'. E ripensavo alla triste voglia di ridere che m'era venuta una volta sentendo dire d'un bimbo (che io sapevo sicuramente adulterino) alla presenza dei legittimi coniugi: – Tutto suo padre! – E la somiglianza era straordinaria, per quella misteriosa legge che i fisiologi chiamano *eredità d'influenza.* Per quella legge il figlio talvolta non somiglia nè al padre nè alla madre, ma somiglia all'uomo che ha avuto con la madre un contatto anteriore alla fecondazione. Una donna maritata in seconde nozze, tre anni dopo la morte del primo marito, genera figli che hanno tutti i lineamenti del marito defunto e non somigliano in nulla a colui che li ha procreati.' Gabriele D'Annunzio, *L'innocente,* 285–86. Translation mine.

13. Francis Galton, *Natural Inheritance,* 12.

14. Barbara Spackman, *Decadent Genealogies: The Rhetoric of Sickness from Baudelaire to D'Annunzio,* 168–83.

15. Otto Weininger, *Geschlacht und Charakter,* 307. Translation of this passage by Barbara Hyams. I am indebted to Alberto Cavaglion's article for pointing out these moments in Weininger's text.

16. Burkhardt, 17.

17. I have adopted the newer spelling of 'antisemitism' rather than the older form 'anti-Semitism,' as the newer one, initiated by the historian James Parks, reflects the fact that antisemitism does not comprise prejudice against all Semites, as the older spelling implies, but instead prejudice specifically against Jews.

18. Cited in Benno Müller-Hill, *Murderous Science,* 81. The Streicher passage is reprinted from J. Streicher, *Deutsche Volksgesundheit aus Blut und Boden,* 1.1.35. I wish to thank both Barbara

Hyams and Arthur Shapiro for bringing this passage to my attention.

19. Sander Gilman, *Jewish Self-Hatred: Antisemitism and the Hidden Language of the Jews,* 206.

20. Ibid., 206.

21. Juan Comas, 'Racial Myths,' 38.

22. For a discussion of the relationship between the marginalized individual and mainstream culture, and the internalization of prejudice, see the introduction to Sander Gilman, *Difference and Pathology: Stereotypes of Sexuality, Race and Madness,* 15–35.

23. Andrea Freud Loewenstein's recent book on the convergence of antisemitism and misogyny in the works of several English writers (*Loathsome Jews and Engulfing Women: Metaphors of Projection in the Works of Wyndham Lewis, Charles Williams, and Graham Greene*) appeared too late to be incorporated into the present study.

Chapter 2: The Logic of Intolerance

1. Ellis, one of Lombroso's followers and admirers, writes in *The Criminal,* xviii: 'We used to chain our lunatics. Our lunatic asylums during the past century have become mental hospitals. Our prisons must now really become what it was long ago said they ought to be, moral hospitals.' Gould points out that indeterminate sentencing – usually seen as liberal – can work both ways: to keep 'born' criminals off the streets for long periods of time for even petty crimes under the assumption that once free they will immediately return to crime and to provide short and therefore 'humane' sentences for those who are what Lombroso would call 'occasional criminals.' See *The Mismeasure of Man,* 140–42.

2. Gould tells us, 'The positivist school campaigned hardest and most successfully for a set of reforms, until recently regarded as enlightened or "liberal," and all involving the principle of indeterminate sentencing.' See *The Mismeasure of Man,* 141.

3. For a discussion of the relevance of these physical signs in the discourse of illness in the late nineteenth century, see Spackman, *Decadent Genealogies.*

4. For more discussion of the role of doctors in criminology, see Leonard D. Savitz's introduction to the reprint edition of *Criminal Man*, v–xx.

5. The most well-known theorist of the substitution of the local priest by the family doctor in Italy is the mid-nineteenth-century doctor and anthropologist Paolo Mantegazza, who advocated the shift as a necessary consequence of a newly elevated status of medical science. Doctors were not only capable of informing a healthier family life but were also *compelled* to do so. This kind of competition over the status of family advisers was emblematic of the conflict between science and religion.

6. Ellis, *The Criminal*, x.

7. Leon Radzinowicz, *In Search of Criminology;* citation reprinted in *Criminal Man*, 1972 ed., ix.

8. See Savitz, introduction to reprint edition, *Criminal Man*. This edition was put together just before Lombroso's death by his daughter Gina Lombroso-Ferrero and is a summary of his theories. Lombroso wrote the introduction to the volume, which was first published in 1911 (two years after his death). Savitz's introduction provides a valuable contextualization of Lombroso's theories within the discipline of criminology. Savitz points out that the issue of whose texts were translated played an important role in the development of American criminology, since most practitioners were unskilled in foreign languages. Lombroso's theories had the most influence in the United States. The Lombrosian school was quickly and frequently translated into English, while the French school was poorly represented in translation, and thus many of the latter texts remained unavailable to American criminologists. See also Robert A. Nye, *Crime, Politics and Madness in Modern France: The Medical Concept of National Decline*, for a discussion of Lombroso's influence.

9. For further discussion of the French school of criminology, see Savitz, introduction to reprint edition of *Criminal Man*, v–xx; and Gould, *The Mismeasure of Man*, chap.4.

10. 'Fra le molte, nuove ricerche dell'antropologia criminale, quella sulla donna delinquente e prostituta, più di qualunque altra riconfermano il vantaggio della cieca osservazione dei fatti . . . I

principali risultati, infatti, a cui fin dalle prime indagini giungemmo, erano in opposizione alle comuni premesse; anche le singole, parziali osservazioni parevano contrastarsi l'una con l'altra: sicchè, chi per amore del sistema avesse voluto essere logico, avrebbe dovuto esitare nelle definitive conclusioni' (v). Cesare Lombroso and Guglielmo Ferrero, *La donna delinquente, la prostituta e la donna normale,* v; all subsequent quotations from Lombroso in this chapter are from this text unless otherwise indicated.

11. 'Ma noi, fedeli alla massima che ci ha sorretti in tutta la vita, abbiamo seguiti ciecamente i fatti, anche quando parevano più contraddirsi fra loro, anche quando parevano cacciarci su una falsa strada. Ne' mal ci apponemmo; perchè, allo stringer delle reti, i fatti più opposti, incastrandosi pei loro angoli come i lapilli di un mosaico, formarono un disegno organico e completo: che se il modo di raccoglierli sulle prime tornò incerto ed uggioso come a chi brancica all'oscuro, quando alla fine ci si asperse una meta lucida e chiara, gustammo l'aspro piacere del cacciatore che acciuffa la preda per balze e discese, e sente raddoppiata la gioia del successo dalle ansie delle perdite e dalle fatiche della conquista.

Non di raro poi questi rimbalzi, come le ondate del mare, ci trascinarono molto più lungi dalla meta prefissa, e, quel ch'è meglio, più in alto, aiutandoci così ad appianare le continue contraddizioni che si affacciavano sin dalle prime linee' (v–vi).

12. See Keller, *Reflections;* and Sandra Harding, *The Science Question in Feminism,* for discussions of androcentrism in science.

13. Keller, *Reflections,* 10.

14. For further information on the history of abduction, see Umberto Eco, 'Horns, Hooves, and Insteps,' 198–220. Carlo Ginzburg, in 'Clues: Morelli, Freud and Sherlock Holmes,' 81–118, discusses the epistemology of the hunt and its connection to the retroactive thinking that is abduction. Both of the above are in Umberto Eco and Thomas Sebeok, eds., *The Sign of Three: Dupin, Holmes, Peirce.*

15. For a discussion of the relationship of the method of Claude Bernard and Peircean abduction, see Nancy Harrowitz, 'The Science of Detection: Epistemology and Materiality in Late Nineteenth Century Italian Mysteries.'

16. 'E neppure si sviluppò dal nulla: poichè diversi decenni prima della pubblicazione del libro principale di Lombroso, *L'uomo delinquente,* nel 1876, i criminali ed i devianti già costituivano oggetto di ricerca e di studio. E tuttavia il panorama delle "scienze dell'uomo" del secolo scorso risulterebbe in qualche modo nebuloso senza quell'opera, ed i suoi significati. Dunque si tratta di ripercorrere – rileggere e ricostruire – un itinerario culturale e, nei suoi tempi, scientifico.' Renzo Villa, *Il deviante ed i suoi segni,* 7–8.

17. Gould, *The Mismeasure of Man,* 126.

18. Just how similar and related – and still very urgent – are some of these issues is discussed at length in Carl N. Degler's recent study, *In Search Of Human Nature: The Decline and Revival of Darwinism in American Social Thought.* Lombroso, as a major proponent of Darwinism, provides yet another link in Darwinian theory that, according to Degler, still influences American social science today.

19. 'Così vedemmo la femmina nelle più basse serie zoologiche essere superiore al maschio in volume, in complicazione degli organi, quasi padrona della specie, per poi calare ad esserne l'umile schiava, menomata in forza, in variabilità, ecc.; e così nella razza nostra essa appare uguale o superiore all'uomo prima della pubertà in forza e statura, spesso in ingegno, ma poi man mano gli resta indietro, lasciando nella stessa momentanea prevalenza una prova di quella precocità che è comune alle razze inferiori' (vi–vii).

20. Cynthia Eagle Russett, *Sexual Science: The Victorian Construction of Womanhood,* 50. See also Gould, *The Mismeasure of Man,* esp. chap.4.

21. Gould, *The Mismeasure of Man,* 51.

22. Ibid., 113–14.

23. Contextualizing Lombroso within nineteenth-century scientific thought is important for two reasons. First, it helps us understand in his theories on women when he is following scientists before him and when he is offering independent ideas. Second, an understanding of the political, cultural, and scientific influences of the time will also help us to avoid the pitfall to which Villa alludes, that of a snobbish cultural relativism.

24. 'Quanto la donna ci possa esser utile e cara, ben lo poterono provare in questo libro stesso quelle egregie signore Mad. Caccia, Mad. dott. Tarnowsky, Mlle Helen Zimmern, Mad. C. Royer, Mad. Rossi, Mad. dott. Kulischoff, che, avendo compreso le mie idee meglio e prima e più estesamente di molti dei nostri pensatori, a questo studio hanno collaborato con documenti, notizie, consigli nelle più difficili direzioni; e tu lo provi più di tutte, mia carissima Gina, l'ultimo e l'unico filo che mi riunisca alla vita, la collaboratrice e l'ispiratrice più salda, più feconda di ogni mio lavoro' (xi).

25. The racism of Lombroso's thought regarding blacks and those whom he calls 'uomini di colore' [men of color] is a separate (but related) issue too complex to be dealt with here. I reiterate that the major point of difference in considering Lombroso's attitudes toward various groups is his personal relationship to them. Degler writes that 'the question of the nature of woman, unlike a similar inquiry regarding blacks, was complicated by greater familiarity and greater complexity. Most male scientists, like the public at large, had close and enduring contact with women and usually almost none with blacks. How one perceived blacks or Indians, or immigrants or women, depended on one's relation to them, for that shaped one's expectations. As early twentieth-century social scientists rightly pointed out, for a dominant group to classify or identify a subordinate group, whether a sex or a race, was, ipso facto, to exert some control over it.' *In Search of Human Nature*, 105.

26. 'Coloro che, nei libri sulla donna, non si contentano della logica serrata dei fatti, ma continuando, o meglio, falsificando le tradizioni medioevali, vogliono anche la cavalleria verso quella parte gentile che più ci infiora la vita, troveranno che, spesso, nella nostra opera, le abbiamo mancato di riguardo. Ma, se non abbiamo portato rispetto ai nostri preconcetti più cari, come all'idea del tipo, del reo-nato, se non abbiamo avuto paura dell'apparente contraddizione che agli occhi volgari avrebbe potuto sembrare deleteria d'ogni nostra opera, come potevamo farci pedissequi a una menzogna convenzionale, punto scientifica, che non acquista una forma che per perderla subito?' (viii).

27. 'Ma non però quelle misure devonsi abbandonare, non fosse

altro come cornice del quadro, come simbolo, come bandiera di una scula che fa della cifra la miglior sua arma, tanto più che quelle poche volte che vi si rinvenga l'anomalia, ne raddoppiano l'importanza' (262).

28. 'L'uomo ama la donna per la vulva, la donna ama nell'uomo il marito e il padre' (57).

29. 'Non una linea di quest'opera quindi giustifica le molte tirannie di cui la donna è stata ed è tuttora vittima: dal Tabù che le vieta di mangiare le carni o di toccare le noci di cocco, fino a quello che le impedisce d'imparare, e peggio, di esercitare una professione una volta imparata: coercizioni ridicole o crudeli, prepotenti sempre, colle quali certo abbiamo contribuito a mantenere, e, quel che è più triste, ad accrescere la inferiorità sua, per sfruttarla a nostro vantaggio, anche quando ipocritamente coprivamo la docile vittima di elogi a cui non credevamo, e che, piuttosto di un ornamento, erano una preparazione a nuovi sacrifizi' (x).

30. Gina Lombroso, in a biography of her father, eulogizes her mother's sacrifices so that her husband and daughters could have careers. This puts a particularly ironic twist on Lombroso's statement regarding man's role in encouraging and exploiting the sacrifices of women. The passage from Gina Lombroso is cited in Villa, *Il deviante ed i suoi segni,* 13.

31. Hilde Olrik, in 'Le sang impur: Notes sur le prostituée de Lombroso,' discusses class distinctions that underlie Lombroso's analysis.

32. 'Quel fondo d'immoralità che latente si trova in ogni donna' (490); 'Quel fondo di malvagità che è latente in ogni donna' (507).

33. 'È chiaro che da quella semi-criminaloide innocua che è la donna normale dovrà escire una criminale-nata più terribile d'ogni delinquente maschio. Che criminali terribili non sarebbero infatti i bambini se avessero grandi passioni, forza e intelligenza, se di più le loro tendenze al male fossero esasperate da una eccitazione morbosa! Ora le donne sono dei grandi bambini; le loro tendenze al male sono più numerose e più svariate che nell'uomo, solo rimangono quasi sempre latenti; quando però sono attizzate e ridestate, il loro risultato è naturalmente assai più grande' (433–34).

34. 'Dimostrare come le menzogna sia abituale e quasi fisio-

logica nella donna sarebbe superfluo, tanto è perfino nella leggenda popolare'; 'le donne dicono sempre il vero, ma non lo dicono mai intero'; 'le donne – dice il Dohm – si servono della bugia come il bue delle corna' (133).

35. 'La maternità è – quasi diremmo – essa stessa un vaccino morale contro il delitto e il male' (499).

36. Charles Bernheimer, in *Figures of Ill-Repute: Representing Prostitution in Nineteenth-Century France,* 259, asserts that 'Lombroso's influential book . . . is permeated with the terror that active – that is, masculinized – female sexuality will cause a catastrophic collapse of sexual difference (hence Lombroso's normative definition of woman as "naturally monogamous and frigid").'

37. 'Ma se la donna primitiva non fu che di raro assassina, fu, come provammo sopra . . ., sempre prostituta, e restò tale quasi fino all'epoca semi-barbara; quindi anche atavisticamente si spiega che la prostituta debba avere più caratteri regressivi della donna criminale' (358). 'Le prostitute riprodurrebbero più atavisticamente la donna primitiva, la Venere vaga' (358–59).

38. 'Si direbbe la laringe di un uomo. E così nella laringe, come nella faccia, come nel cranio, spicca il carattere speciale a queste, la virilità' (334); 'distribuzione virile del pelo' (330).

39. 'Però, anche nelle ree più belle il carattere virile, l'esagerazione della mascella, degli zigomi, non manca mai, come non manca in nessuna delle nostre grandi cocottes, sicchè hanno tutte un'aria di famiglia che avvicina le peccatrici Russe a quelle che stancano le vie delle nostre città, sieno esse in cocchi dorati o in umili cenci. E fate che la giovinezza scompaia, e allora quelle mandibole, quegli zigomi arrotondati dall'adipe, sporgono gli angoli salienti e ne rendono il viso affatto virile, più brutto di un uomo, e la ruga si approfonda come una ferita, e quella faccia piacente mostra completamente il tipo degenerato che l'età nascondeva' (350).

40. Olrik, 'Le sang impur,' 167.

41. See Janice Delaney, Mary Jane Lupton, and Emily Toth, *The Curse: A Cultural History of Menstruation,* esp. chap.4.

42. Ibid., pp.38–39; they also give an example of the defense of the laws of *niddah* given by an Orthodox Jewish woman who is also a feminist.

43. This enforced segregation of women continued into early Christian times and became a subject of debate among Christian theologians who finally for the most part dismissed any cultural relevancy of menstruation. The taboo thus weakened over time, although Delaney et al., ibid., point out that arguments against women's involvement in the Church on the basis of the menstrual taboos in Leviticus were still used as recently as 1970.

44. 'E della menzogna le donne non hanno vergogna; la dicono senza arrossire; le più elette di spirito se ne servono con perfetta sicurezza per intenti pietosi' (135).

45. 'In molte lingue la parola *giuramento, testimonianza* si riconnette con testicolo (es.: . . . in latino *testis*)' (136). The Zingarelli Italian dictionary gives the etymology of *testimonio* [witness] as ' "deposizione del teste (*testis*)", passata poi dal senso astratto a quello concreto' [deposition of the witness (*testis*), moving from the abstract sense to the concrete].

46. 'Quando la mestruazione divenne un oggetto di ribrezzo per l'uomo, la donna deve nasconderla. Anche oggi è questa la prima bugia che si insegna alla donna; la si ammaestra a nascondere il proprio stato con la simulazione di altri mali. Ora ciò vuol dire costringere ogni mese la donna a due o tre giorni di menzogne continue, vale a dire un esercizio di dissimulazione periodico' (136).

47. 'Il pudore – scrive Stendhal – ha questo svantaggio, che abitua a mentire' (136). *Pudore* translates as more than mere 'modesty'; it involves a sense of right and wrong and an accompanying sense of either real or imagined shame. However, so as not to overencumber the text, I will hereforth translate it as 'modesty.'

48. 'E se il pudore discende da *putere,* si vede facilmente come sino dai suoi primordi dovesse abituare alla bugia' (136).

49. 'La donna è, in conclusione, un grande fanciullo, e i fanciulli sono i mentitori per eccellenza. E tanto più facilmente mentiscono le donne che le ragioni della menzogna sono per loro più numerose che per essi' (139).

50. 'E si capisce come la chiacchiera del delitto sia più frequente nella donna che nell'uomo, perchè essa deve supplire a tutti quei mezzi usati dal maschio a ravvivare l'immagine del delitto, come il

disegno e la scrittura, che vedemmo mancare alla donna. La donna parla spesso de' suoi delitti, come l'uomo li dipinge, o li scrive, o li scolpisce nei vasi, ecc.' (465).

51. 'Un minor sviluppo del centro grafico' (175).

52. Gilman, *Jewish Self-Hatred*, 14.

Chapter 3: Vilifying Difference

1. 'Ne provavo quel disgusto che coglie anche il meno impaziente scienziato quando deve studiare le più ributtanti secrezioni umane. Il decidere se un odio fra popoli possa essere giustificato, nei nostri tempi, è già certo un odioso e doloroso compito; e non è agevole acconciarvisi.' Cesare Lombroso, *L'antisemitismo e le scienze moderne*, 5; all citations from Lombroso in this chapter are from this text unless otherwise indicated.

2. 'Mi garantiva anche contro il pericolo, massimo in tali quistioni, della parzialità' (6); 'l'aiuto di tali mastri sorti nelle nazioni più ricche di antisemiti e di filosemiti mi era nuova arra della rettitudine e dell'imparzialità del giudizio per chi dubitasse dello strumento che da poco tempo maneggio' (7).

3. 'La segregazione dell'abitato, la dissonanza degli usi, dei cibi, dei dialetti, la concorrenza nei commerci che fomentava gelosie, aumentava disparità reali e apparenti, rendendo desiderabile ed utile ai privati, se non al paese, il loro avvilamento; e infine la epidemia psichica che diffonde e centuplica gli odi e le leggende' (12).

4. 'Certo contribuì pure alla persecuzione il carattere degli stessi perseguitati' (13).

5. See Michael Seltzer, ed., *Kike! Antisemitism in America*, for further antisemitic descriptions and stereotypes.

6. 'Gli stupidi riti delle azime Pasquali; i quali, divergendo da tutti quelli in uso fra i popoli in cui vivono, destano naturalmente il ridicolo e la ripugnanza che cresce coll'esagerata importanza che gli ortodossi vi annettono' (14).

7. 'L'uso di legarsi al braccio, alla testa, dei pezzi di cuio contenenti alcune formole religiose (per esempio, Dio è unico), rimonta certo all'epoca in cui la parola scritta, inventata da poco, assumeva

presso i più un'importanza maravigliosa, un significato simbolico, mistico, per cui si credeva quasi che una formola scritta facesse miracoli. Ora che fin gli ultimi portinai leggono migliaia di righe in un giorno nei giornali, una formola scritta che si tenga per qualche cosa di magico fa ridere, o desta l'idea di tristi misteri. Il peggio è che essi rimontano ancora più su; il vero ortodosso Ebreo (fortunatamente ve ne sono pochi) giunge a qualcosa di più strano, a portare ricami nei suoi manti religiosi gli avanzi di quei veri guippi o nodi mnemonici in filo che avevano gli uomini primitivi, I Peruviani per esempio, prima della scrittura ideografica, prima dell'alfabeto a pittura' (7).

8. For a discussion of the role and function of tefillin in Judaism, see Aryeh Kaplan, *Tefillin*.

9. For a discussion of relics, see P. R. L. Brown, *Relics and Social Status in the Age of Gregory of Tours*.

10. Gilman, *Jewish Self-Hatred*, ix.

11. Ibid., 20.

12. 'Convengo tuttavia che la maggioranza loro non è morale, e sente più la bramosità e l'avidità del potere che quella del bene: ma questo pure si spiega con l'andazzo dell'epoca nostra. Rappresentando la modernità, essi, pur troppo, ne portano le piaghe' (100).

13. In Lombroso's discussions of the physical signs of criminality in his works on female and male 'delinquents,' he in fact uses the word *stigmata* to point out these physical differences.

14. 'Chesojub, che la Russia ha spento, ma che il mondo adora quale un Cristo novello' (100).

15. 'Modernity' in fact can be read as 'capitalism,' as Lombroso the socialist has here made modernity synonymous with the economic struggles of capitalism.

16. 'Una stigmata grave di degenerazione è in molte criminalinate la mancanza dell'affetto materno' (435).

17. 'Agli ebrei a lor volta tocca persuadersi come molti dei loro riti ormai appartengono ad altre epoche e per le loro inutili stranezze (azime, p. es.; circoncisione) fanno sospettare ai profani di costumi di cui essi stessi hanno il massimo ribrezzo. Se tutte le religioni hanno modificato le loro essenza, non che la loro veste, a seconda dei tempi, perchè non dovrebbero modificarne essi al-

meno la vernice? Perché non rinunciare a quel vero ferimento selvaggio che è la circoncisione, a quei molteplici feticci della scrittura sacra o di alcuni dei suoi periodi, che essi spargono nelle proprie case e persino legano sopra il proprio corpo, precisamente come gli amuleti, conservando senza saperlo quell'adorazione delle lettere che ne ebbero i primi scopritori e che hanno ancora i selvaggi?' (107).

18. Mezuzahs are small objects containing an important prayer from the book of Deuteronomy placed on the doorframes of Jewish homes.

19. Steven Beller, *Vienna and the Jews, 1867–1938,* 208.

20. It seems clear that Lombroso and Herzl have some aspects in common: both grew up in somewhat assimilated Jewish families, both were fascinated by the culture of their country, and both seemed to absorb some of the antisemitic attitudes of the day. For a discussion of the life of Herzl that touches on his relationship to his own upbringing as a Jew, see Amos Elon, *Herzl.*

21. Jacob Katz assesses various kinds of reactions to antisemitism in the second half of the nineteenth century on the part of the Jewish community in *From Prejudice to Destruction: Antisemitism, 1700–1933,* esp. 4–6. Another writer who posited assimilation as the solution to the 'Jewish question' was Maurice Fishberg, who in *The Jews: A Study of Race and Environment* asserts, like Lombroso, that the Jews were not a race.

22. Katz, among others, has discussed the anticlerical and antisemitic aspects of liberalism in *From Prejudice to Destruction,* esp. chap. 10.

23. 'Un altro bacillo epidemico' (24); 'i germi del morbo' (26).

24. 'Ma le scienze naturali ci dimostrano che l'evoluzione non è mai completa, e che sempre ad una grande evoluzione in una direzione si accompagna un arresto in altre direzioni; e noi vediamo, infatti, popoli straordinariamente progrediti in una direzione presentare straordinarie regressioni in altre. Così gli Ebrei che andarono con Cristo fino al comunismo, con Mosè al monoteismo, con Marx al socialismo, che crearono la cambiale, formarono il nucleo della borghesia capitalista, come ora inalberano il quarto stato contro questa, che si trovarono insomma presenti ed atti a

tutte le evoluzioni più avanzate, pure non solo perdettero il corag-
gio personale e l'energia patriottica che aveva fatto meravigliare
fino il romano collo spettacolo di una intera città suicidatasi tutta
piuttosto che arrendersi, ma adottano ancora religiosamente i
guippu (alfabeto a nodi) nel loro *taled,* e le armi di pietra nella
circoncisione, e conservano in questa un avanzo del cannibalismo;
in politica poi mostrarono sempre un eccesso di conservatismo.
Appena si fissarono per qualche tempo in un paese ne conservano
le usanze, perfino i vestiti quando questi erano già scomparsi nel
paese originario; qualche volta perfino la lingua.' *Genio de degenerazione: nuovi studi e nuove battaglie,* 13–14.

25. 'Giunge ad adoperare nella crudele pratica della circoncisione insieme ai denti i coltelli di pietra come i nostri proavi della
caverne' (7).

26. Bram Stoker, *Dracula,* 346. This citation is also found in
Gould, *The Mismeasure of Man,* 123, and in Clive Leatherdale,
Dracula: The Novel and the Legend, 210.

27. Leonard Wolf, *Annotated Dracula,* 300. Reprinted in
Gould, *Mismeasure of Man,* 123, and Leatherdale, *Dracula,* 211.

28. Sander Gilman, ' "I'm Down on Whores": Race and Gender
in Victorian London,' 156.

29. Arthur Shapiro has brought to my attention the argument
made by Paul Barker in *Vampires, Burial and Death* (1988) that
the typical vampire found in folklore before Stoker, Nosferatu, etc.
was not a 'semitic' type, but rather one that resembled an Eastern
European peasant.

30. Ellis, *The Criminal,* xi.

31. Lombroso came from a clearly identified, although probably
somewhat assimilated, Jewish family. The only reference I have
been able to find regarding the precise nature of the religious identification of Lombroso's family is in Renzo Villa's book, when in
an aside he mentions the fact that the members of Lombroso's
family were atheists. Only from a strictly religious point of view is
this fact – if it is true – significant. It is much less significant in
trying to establish the cultural identity of the family and their
cultural affiliations in a time when liberalism was popular especially among intellectual Jewish families. This situation often re-

sulted in individuals who were not religious but were strongly identified as Jews nonetheless.

32. 'Presso gli Ebrei, prima della redazione definitiva delle tavole della legge, il padre aveva diritto di vendere la figlia ad un padrone che ne facesse la propria concubina per un tempo stabilito dal contratto di vendita: e la figlia venduta in quel modo per profitto di suo padre, non ricavava alcun vantaggio personale dall'abbandono forzato del proprio corpo, tranne il caso in cui il padrone, dopo averla fidanzata al proprio figlio, volesse sostituirla con un' altra concubina. Gli Ebrei trafficavano insomma della prostituzione delle loro figlie' (226).

33. The model for this sort of father-daughter exploitation does exist: as Robert Oden tells us in 'Religious Identity and the Sacred Prostitution Accusation,' the Greek historian Herodotus, the source for most of the information on cultic and sacred prostitution, 'refers in passing to the Lydian custom by which parents turn their daughters into prostitutes who thereby earn dowries for themselves' (141). This is a similar, if not exact rendition of Lombroso's version regarding the Jews, since here the Lydian daughters end up with a dowry. Herodotus influenced most of the other early writers and thinkers on the topic of sacred prostitution, and Lombroso was probably familiar with his work either directly or indirectly. This possible source for a similar story does not of course explain why Lombroso would attribute this tradition to the Jews instead of the Lydians.

34. Sander Gilman, ' "I'm Down on Whores": Race and Gender in Victorian London,' 161.

35. 'Tra gli Ebrei, però, prima delle riforme mosaiche, la prostituzione sacra era enormemente diffusa; anzi l'opera legislativa di Mosè fu soprattutto una lotta contro i culti fallici di Moloch e di Baal-Fegor, comuni alle popolazioni semitiche. Mosè tentò di estirpare la prostituzione religiosa; ma non vi riuscì, perché tracce di prostituzione religiosa troviamo nei libri santi fino all'epoca dei Maccabei. . . . (224) Tali; gli eccessi deg'Israeliti con le donzelle Moabite che si collegano ad un culto fallico. Queste donzelle avevano innalzate delle tende ed aperte delle botteghe (officine) da Bet-Aiscimot insino ad Ar-Ascaleg: là esse vendevano ogni sorta di

gioielli, e gli Ebrei mangiavano e bevevano nel mezzo di questo
campo di prostituzione (Numeri, XXV). Il profeta Ezechiello ci
lasciò una dipintura spaventevole della corruzione ebraica; non
altro vi si legge che di cortegiane vestite di seta e di ricami, scin-
tillanti di gioielli e cosperse di profumi, e dappertutto scene infami
di fornicazione.

Il tempio di Gerusalemme all'epoca dei Maccabei, un secolo e
mezzo prima di Gesù Cristo, era ancora il teatro del commercio
delle prostitute che venivano a cercarvi le loro pratiche' (225–26).

36. Cultic or sacred prostitution, taken for granted as a historical reality by scholars since Herodotus, has now been challenged
by some scholars as an 'accusation' with an accompanying ideological agenda. Little if any empirical evidence exists to prove that
it ever took place. For two discussions of this topic, the first maintaining that this practice has no historical validity and the second
attempting to 'prove' that it existed but in fact demonstrating the
paucity of evidence, see Robert Oden, 'Religious Identity and the
Sacred Prostitution Accusation'; and Edwin M. Yamauchi, 'Cultic
Prostitution: A Case Study in Cultural Diffusion.'

37. 'Mosè per tranquillizzare i mariti che sospettavano le spose,
malate di blenorragia, di adulterio, ordinò, quando la moglie im-
putasse del suo male il marito, che ambedue andassero davanti al
sagrificatore; il marito offriva per la moglie una focaccia di farina
d'orzo senz'olio, chiamata focaccia della gelosia; il sagrificatore
poneva la focaccia sulle mani della donna e serbava nelle proprie la
acque amare che recavano la maledizione: "Se nessun uomo ha
dormito teco, diceva il prete, e se essendo sottoposta a tuo marito
non t'imbrattasti, sii esente da queste acque amare; ma se essendo
accaduto il contrario, tu fosti impura e fornicasti con altri, che
l'Eterno ti abbandoni all'esecrazione alla quale sei soggetta con
giuramento, e queste acque di maledizione entrino nelle tue viscere
per farti gonfiare il ventre ed essiccare la coscia." La donna rispon-
deva amen, e beveva le acque amare. Se alla donna più tardi gon-
fiava il ventre ed essiccava la coscia, era convinta d'adulterio e
diveniva infame agli occhi d'Israele. Il marito, per l'opposto, che
tutti compiangevano come una vittima innocente, trovavasi giustificato, se non guarito' (191–92).

Chapter 4: Portraits of Self-Abnegation

1. Robert Oden, 'Religious Identity and the Sacred Prostitution Accusation,' 132–33.

2. For further discussion of the Jews after the ghettos, see Jacob Katz, *Out of the Ghetto.* For other interesting discussions of Jewish self-hatred, see Jack Nusan Porter, *The Jew as Outsider,* and Allan Janik, "Viennese Culture and the Jewish Self-Hatred Hypothesis: A Critique."

3. Paul Marcus and Alan Rosenberg, "Another Look at Jewish Self-Hatred," citations from 37, 42, 50.

4. Leonard Glick, 'Types Distinct from Our Own: Franz Boas on Jewish Identity and Assimilation,' 546.

5. Ibid.

6. Franz Boas, *Race and Democratic Society,* 81. Reprinted in Glick, 'Types Distinct,' 557.

7. Franz Boas, 'An Anthropologist's Credo,' 201–2. Reprinted in Glick, 'Types Distinct,' 555.

8. Glick, 'Types Distinct,' 545.

9. For debates regarding the racism apparent in the term *race,* see Gates, ed. *'Race,' Writing and Difference,* esp. 1–20; and Anthony Appiah, 'The Uncompleted Argument: Du Bois and the Illusion of Race,' 21–37.

10. There are several critical texts that confront Weininger's influence on European literature, e.g., Jacques Le Rider's *Le cas Otto Weininger: racines de l'antiféminisme et l'antisémitisme,* and forthcoming essays on Weininger and writers such as Canetti, Joyce and Kafka: Nancy Harrowitz and Barbara Hyams, eds., *Jews and Gender: Responses to Otto Weininger.*

11. Otto Weininger, *Sex and Character,* 303.

12. Ibid., 304.

13. Jeffrey Mehlman, review of Sander Gilman's *Jewish Self-Hatred: Antisemitism and the Hidden Language of the Jews,* 668.

14. See Allan Janik, *How Not to Interpret a Culture: Essays on the Problem of Method in the Geisteswissenshaften,* 37, for further explanation of this point.

15. Weininger, *Sex and Character,* 306.

16. Ibid., 306, 307, 309, 311.

17. I am indebted to Barbara Spackman's chapter on Lombroso, in *Decadent Genealogies: The Rhetoric of Sickness From Baudelaire to D'Annunzio,* esp. 29–30, for the term *degenderation.*

18. Ibid., 9.

19. For discussion of the feminized male Jew, see John Hoberman, 'The Myth of Jewish Effeminacy.'

20. For more discussion of this point, see Cavaglion, *Otto Weininger in Italia.*

21. Janik, *How Not to Interpret a Culture,* 40.

22. Ibid., 36.

23. For a discussion of the ways in which liberalism has been associated with antisemitism, see Ruth R. Wisse, *If I Am Not for Myself: The Liberal Betrayal of the Jews,* esp. 21–42.

24. See ibid., 27–56.

25. 'Nel capitolo sul Giudaismo, dopo aver affermato che l'ebreo manca assolutamente di fede, in sè e nel mondo esterno, spiega come tuttavia precisamente dal Giudaismo possa nascere il Cristo, perchè "il fondatore di religione è quell'uomo il quale è vissuto totalmente senza Dio, e pur nondimeno è riuscito a conquistarsi la fede." Senza dubbio il Weininger patì dell'incertezza radicale che egli attribuisce all'ebreo e volle conquistarsi una fede.' Giulio Augusto Levi, 'Ottone Weininger,' 261.

Chapter 5: Matilde Serao and the Body of Passion

1. One index of her exclusion from the canon is that, even though she was one of the most popular and prolific novelists and journalists of the past century, there is no article dedicated to her in the well-known three-volume reference work, *Dizionario critico della letteratura italiana,* that purportedly covers all major and almost all minor writers.

2. Croce was one of Serao's admirers, remarking about the writing in one of her stories, 'Così calda, rapida, vivace è quest'arte della Serao. Sembra che il suo stile abbia assorbito l'eloquio abbondante, il gesticolare espressivo, l'affolarsi dei colori forti, l'emozionalità subitanea ed irrefrenabile ch'è nella vita e nelle creature che essa ritrae.' [So warm, quick and vivacious is this art

of Serao's. It seems that her style has absorbed the abundant speech, the expressive gesturing, the crowding of strong colors, the unexpected and uncontrollable emotion which is in the life and creatures that she depicts.] From 'Note sulla letteratura italiana nella seconda metà del secolo XIX,' 332. Croce does not by any means laud all of Serao's works in this lengthy review article. He divides them into categories including works of verismo, what he calls 'i drammi della passione,' i.e., 'sentimental' novels that are mixed with an interest in verismo, and some of her later works, which show interest in mysticism. The first two categories are by and large acclaimed by Croce, while the last does not, according to him, represent Serao's best inspiration.

3. Gramsci's oft-quoted analysis of the appeal of popular fiction, 'un sognare ad occhi aperti' [dreaming with eyes open] (*Letteratura e vita nazionale,* 108), has greatly contributed to the current level of prejudice and disdain regarding this kind of fiction. Marxist criticism has analyzed popular fiction mostly from the point of view of its ideological structures and has almost entirely ignored it as literature per se. Most other forms of criticism have not considered popular literature to be worthy of consideration. In reviewing how critics before Gramsci viewed Serao's work, it is important to keep in mind that, at the turn of the century, these strong and uniform critical prejudices toward popular fiction did not yet exist.

4. One example among many is found in Anthony Gisolfi, *The Essential Matilde Serao,* who states that Serao's later work (which almost exclusively concentrated on themes of female psychology, eroticism, and love) was unworthy of critical attention. This artificial categorization of Serao's novels does not take into account the subtleties of her fiction.

5. Serao was in fact a friend of Lombroso's, according to Isabella Pezzini in *Carolina Inverzinio, Matilde Serao, Liala: Tre donne attorno al cuore,* 75. Pezzini informs us that Serao even adopts Lombroso's critical vocabulary in one of her stories as she talks about the 'moral type' of woman.

6. For an analysis of many of Serao's newspaper editorials and a summary of her journalistic career, see Wanda De Nunzio Schilardi, *Matilde Serao giornalista.*

7. Serao's biography is fascinating, especially when we consider her literary and journalistic productivity: she had four sons with her husband and then a daughter at age 48 with her companion Giuseppe Natale.

8. For example, see Umberto Eco, Maria Federzoni, Isabella Pezzini, and Maria Pia Pozzato, *Carolina Invernizio, Matilde Serao, Liala*. Ursula Fanning, 'Angel vs. Monster: Serao's Use of the Female Double,' places Serao's work within the tradition of the double, usually analyzed in works by male authors. Through her analysis of the primacy of female relationships in Serao, Fanning is situating her as an author whose interests lie at the edge of feminist concerns.

9. Lucienne Kroha, *The Woman Writer in Late Nineteenth-Century Italy: Gender and the Formation of Literary Identity*, 4–5.

10. Kroha, *The Woman Writer*, 4, letter of Verga cited in F. Bruni, introduction to M. Serao, *Il romanzo della fanciulla*, X.

11. Ursula Fanning, 'Sentimental Subversion: Representations of Female Friendships in the Work of Matilde Serao.'

12. Ibid., 285; italics are mine.

13. The case of Serao as a woman writer who wrote against feminism yet was obviously concerned about women's issues is by no means unique. See, e.g., Lucienne Kroha's discussion of Neera (Anna Radius Zuccari) in *The Woman Writer*, 67–86.

14. Deanna Shemek defines Serao's use of passion by stating, 'The images she builds around a recurrent theme of debilitating passion constitute Serao's coherent, and ambivalent, view of the limits and consequences of women's desire.' Shemek, 'Prisoners of Passion: Women and Desire in Matilde Serao's Romanzi D'Amore.' Croce speaks of the theme of passion in Serao's *Cuore infermo* as the central concern of the novel.

15. *Cuore infermo* appeared in 1881 when Serao was twenty-three years old.

16. 'Ella amava e taceva: il cuore le diceva: io sono infermo, io non posso sopportare tutto questo, io ne morirò – ed ella soffocava anche questa voce . . . la notte talvolta, quando le ansietà si accumulavano, il palpito del cuore diventava precipitoso, il respiro si

affannava, il volto diventava terreo, le mani si gonfiarono . . .
dicono che accogliesse molto bene la donna per cui era tradita, che
la baciasse anche.' Matilde Serao, *Cuore infermo,* 115.

17. 'Queste malattie del cuore si ereditano, come la tisi e la
follia' (115).

18. Susan Sontag, *Illness as Metaphor,* 5.

19. Ibid., 8.

20. Ibid., 11.

21. 'gli si arrovesciò nelle braccia, senza una parola, pallida e
muta di passione' (243).

22. Sontag, *Illness as Metaphor,* 38.

23. The disease and its displacement in this early Serao novel
also signal a late-romantic category in the representation of illness.

24. 'E' proprio lei la donna moderna, la donna appassionata,
strana, forse superficiale, delicata, ammalata, nervosa, capric-
ciosa, dalle apparenze varie che tutti seducono; la donna fatta per
piacere alla inquieta e raffinata gioventù moderna' (113).

25. 'Il loro strano amore era cominciato nel nome di Beatrice, lei
lontana. Per diletto malsano, Lalla si era compiaciuta di gettarlo
spesso in viso a Marcello, come una sferzata, nel più alto momento
della passione; se ne era compiaciuta maggiormente, perché ella
stessa sentiva nel petto il contraccolpo di quel dolore' (147).

26. 'Non vi è propriamente una malattia letale, che si chia-
mi passione; i medici antichi e moderni non la conoscono, non
l'hanno mai trovata, facendo l'autopsia del cadavere. Ma la passione è così sottile ingannatrice, che ella è in fondo di tutte le
malattie mortali. Essa è nella tisi che fa agonizzare per anni coloro
che amano troppo, che non furono abbastanza amati; essa è nei
mali del cuore, in quel cuore che si dilata sotto l'onda dell'emo-
zione passionale, che si serra nella disperazione; essa è nelle lunghe
anemie, che distruggono il corpo umano, fibra per fibra, gelandone
l'epidermide, spezzandone ogni energia; essa è nella nevrosi che fa
tremare di freddo e divampare in un calore insopportabile, che
attacca ora il cervello, ora lo stomaco, che fa battere i denti
per freddo mortale e che torce tutti i nervi in un crampo che fa
impazzire . . . non si muore di tisi, di anemia d'ipertrofia, di nevrosi; si muore, veramente, per una sola ragione.' Matilde Serao,
Addio amore!, 206–7.

27. 'Al terzo giorno le striature rosse delle guance, delle tempia, si eran fatte di un rosso vivido; sul collo, sulle mani, sulle braccia eran comparse delle macchioline di un rosso accesso, . . . in breve tutta la pelle ebbe queste vivide macchie e la febbre purpurea si dichiarò in tutta la sua veemenza. Vale a dire che il sangue troppo ricco, troppo ardente, troppo precipitoso, aveva così fortemente scosso i tessuti delle vene che . . . tutto il bollente sangue era venuto sotto la pelle . . . al sesto giorno queste macchie si gonfiarono, divennero nerastre . . . ruppero l'epidermide, in più punti, e lasciarono sgorgare un sangue nerastro . . . Anna pareva sputasse sangue, pareva piangesse sangue; pareva che le sue mani, torturate, come quelle di Gesù, stillassero sangue' (59).

28. Childbirth fever was endemic from the middle of the seventeenth century until the beginning of this century.

29. It is already a commonplace that images of ill and convalescent women abound in nineteenth-century literature. For a detailed study that contextualizes the significance of illness in the decadent period, see Spackman, *Decadent Genealogies*.

30. Marina Warner, *Alone of All Her Sex: The Myth and the Cult of the Virgin Mary*, 73.

31. For a discussion of Victorian interpretations of menstruation and its relevance to the image of woman, see Sally Shuttleworth, 'Female Circulation: Medical Discourse and Popular Advertising in the Mid-Victorian Era.'

32. There is an interesting connection between this portrayal of Anna as a suffering religious figure and techniques suggested by Right-wing women writers like Anita Bryant and Ruth Carter Stapleton discussed by Andrea Dworkin in *Right-Wing Women*. A technique of religious displacement of the figure of Jesus onto the insufferable husband is suggested as an aid to 'help' women live through a difficult marriage. Dworkin provides the following example: 'In *The Gift of Inner Healing*, Ruth Carter Stapleton counsels a young woman who is in a desperately unhappy marriage: "Try to spend a little time each day visualizing Jesus coming in the door from work. Then see yourself walking up to him, embracing him. Say to Jesus, 'It's good to have you home Nick'"' (23).

33. 'Noi vedemmo infatti che l'amore per la donna è una specie

di schiavitù accettata con entusiasmo, un sacrificio fatto disin-
teressatamente di tutta se stessa all'amante' (514); 'La pura e
grande passione per se stessa conduce la donna innamorata più al
suicidio od alla pazzia che al delitto; se conduce al delitto è segno
che essa ha potuto sprigionare un fondo latente di cattiveria, o che
la virilità del carattere dava alle veementi passioni i mezzi del delitto che una donna interamente donna non avrebbe mai com-
piuto. Il vero reato adunque per passione d'amore è nella donna –
se reato si può chiamare – il suicidio; gli altri reati invece non sono
per lo più che forme ibride' (516); Lombroso and Ferrero, *La
donna delinquente, la prostituta e la donna normale*.

34. 'Tu non l'ami Hermione Darlington, perchè la invochi?
Luigi, addio . . . la tua donna è nella tomba . . . tu non puoi amare
che Anna ed ella è morta, è morta; non puoi amare che lei, nel
ricordo del passato, nella tomba . . . non ti resta che a far aprire la
cappella di casa Dias e a coricarti, come Amleto, nella tomba di
Anna. Questo ti resta: va, va, addio.' Matilde Serao, *Castigo*, 244–
45.

35. Fanning, in 'Angel vs. Monster,' explores the ways in which
Serao takes the structure of the double typically employed by male
novelists and uses it in her novels about women in order to show
the ambivalences and conflicts apparent in the female role in patriarchy. She analyzes *Addio amore!* as a story of a doubling between Anna and Laura, examining their close relationship in the
first novel and Laura's assumption of Anna's role as Cesare's wife
in the sequel *Castigo*. This analysis is interesting but not entirely
convincing, as it neglects the important role that Hermione plays
in *Castigo*. Fanning's basic point, however, is well taken regarding
the notion of the double and its importance. As Fanning says of the
double, 'Women writers found a way to portray the complete female character, by splitting it into two very different characters,
one socially acceptable, the other unacceptable' (64).

36. Kroha, *The Woman Writer*, 113.

37. Dworkin, *Right-Wing Women*, 13–36.

38. Ibid., 29.

39. Barbara Johnson, *A World of Difference*, 153.

40. 'Avete mai pensato, o suffragette, che la massa delle donne è

di una ignoranza veramente crassa? Avete mai pensato che questa massa di donne ignoranti, non fa nulla per diminuire la propria ignoranza, non legge un giornale, non apre un libro, non si interessa [che] alle conversazioni che escano dal piccolo pettegolezzo? Avete mai pensato che questa massa femminile è impermeabile alle idee e alle conoscenze, che essa rifugge dal pensare, dal riflettere e dal giudicare? . . . Guardatevi bene, suffragette, dal voler spiegare loro la legge communale e provinciale . . . così come si fa negli asili, coi bimbi, fate imparare loro una lezioncina sommaria, e poi, fatevela ripetere. Una specie di catechismo a botta e risposta.' From 'Ma che fanno le femministe?' Reprinted in Wanda D. Nunzio Schilardi's *Matilde Serao giornalista,* 223. There appears to be a word, *che,* missing in the reprinted version of this editorial, which I have inserted in brackets.

41. In an editorial entitled 'La politica femminile,' Serao outlines the reasons why women avoid politics and uses as examples two woman doctors. One is the socialist and feminist Anna Kulischioff, who is refused the right to practice medicine at the hospital in Padua. Serao approves of this expulsion and explains that Kulischioff's 'defect,' as Serao calls it, is that she speaks her mind about politics. Serao compares her to another doctor, a *medichessa,* who is described as tranquil and apolitical and who is esteemed in her profession. The message here and in other Serao editorials regarding professions for women is that, if women are going to engage in professions, they should be quiet, meek, and nonthreatening (emphasized here by the use of the diminutive term *medichessa* for the second doctor). For further discussion, see Wanda De Nunzio Schilardi, 'L'antifemminismo di Matilde Serao.'

42. 'Io so, come tante altre donne sanno, che, come sono composte le leggi nella società moderna, non v'è felicità possibile per la donna, in qualunque condizione essa si trovi: né nel matrimonio, né nell'amore libero, né nell'amore illegale . . . e so anche, come tante altre donne sanno, che tutto si dovrebbe mutare nella società, nel cuore degli uomini e nei fatti umani . . . e so che nessuno muterà tutto e che, allora non vale la pena di mutare niente.' Reprinted in Schilardi, 'L'antifemminismo di Matilde Serao,' 277.

Chapter 6: Who Is the Other?

1. Sander Gilman, *Difference and Pathology: Stereotypes of Sexuality, Race and Madness,* 17–18.

2. Matilde Serao, 'Telegrafi dello stato.'

3. 'Per il largo salone, Cristina Juliano le raggiunse, le salutò, senza fermarsi. Sembrava un brutto uomo vestito da donna, col suo gran corpo sconquassato, troppo largo di spalle, troppo lungo di busto, senza fianchi, con le mani grandi, i polsi nodosi e i piedi enormi. Portava ancora il cappello di paglia bianca, dell'estate, abbassato sulla fronte per mitigare lo spavento che produceva il suo occhio guercio, bianco, pauroso: e per scoprire la dovizia meravigliosa di due treccioni neri, una ricchezza strabocchevole di capelli, che le tiravano la testa indietro, pel peso' (12).

4. 'La prima, Rachele Levi, una israelita, piccola, bruttissima, sempre piena di gioelli, scrisse che avrebbe ogni giorno prestato un'ora di più di servizio' (37).

5. One could argue that the exclusion of Rachele from the private meetings that organized resistance to the extra unpaid work has thus backfired: Why should she then resist? Her exclusion from the meetings shows her marginalization, and the fact that she does not resist shows the effects of this exclusion.

6. See Jacobus, Keller, and Shuttleworth, eds. *Body Politics,* for studies regarding the relationship of the female body to science and culture.

7. Parts of this chapter are significantly revised from sections of my article, 'Matilde Serao's *La mano tagliata:* Figuring the Material in Mystery.'

8. Lynn Gunzberg's recent book, *Strangers at Home: Jews in the Italian Literary Imagination,* gives examples of an antisemitic figuring of the Jew in authors as diverse as Bresciani and Invernizio. Her penetrating study goes a long way toward exploding the commonly held belief that there is little or no tradition of antisemitism in Italian culture.

9. Charles Sanders Peirce's logical category of 'abduction' has been pinpointed by some critics as the specific method by which the detective links physical and semantic traces together into a

hypothesis. For discussions and analyses, see Umberto Eco and Thomas Sebeok, ed. *The Sign of Three: Dupin, Holmes, Peirce.*

10. Shemek, in 'Prisoners of Passion: Women and Desire in Matilde Serao's Romanzi D'Amore,' groups *La mano tagliata* with other novels that she analyzes from the point of view of female passion. I would disagree on this important point: the female characters of the novel are involved to some degree in a sentimental life, particularly Rachele, Maria's daughter, who is in love with Ranieri, but it is specifically male desire that drives the novel and causes the principal action of the plot.

11. 'Sopra un morbido letto di velluto nero, posava una mano femminile ingemmata. Non solo la mano, precisamente: ma anche un pezzo di braccio, troncato quattro dita sotto il gomito. La mano e il pezzo di braccio posavano nel senso della lunghezza della cassetta: il coperchio, anche di velluto imbottito, ne seguiva tutta la forma e combaciava sopr'essa, come l'astuccio di un gioiello. . . . La mano tagliata e ingemmata era bellissima. Lunga con le dita affusolate e separate, come quella dell'amante del divino Raffaello, aveva le linee perfette. Era anche posata artisticamente, col polso appoggiato al velluto, con la palma leggermente sollevata e la punta delle dita appena appoggiate, in una giacitura composta, lieve, quasi immateriale. Le unghie, rosee, lucide, riflettevano il chiarore della lampada: erano lunate e tagliate a mandorla: l'orlo della carne se ne staccava, con eleganza. La mano non era né rosea, né bianca: era color carne, color naturale . . . mano di tinta viva, di persona che era giovane, bella e sana: nulla di esangue, di cereo, di oscuro, in quella mano . . . così pura di forma, di parere statuaria, se non avesse conservato quel colore di carne così parlante, dirò.' Matilde Serao, *La mano tagliata,* 1:31–32.

12. 'Non era grassa e rotonda, come certe mani belline e stupide: né magra, come certe mani che hanno travagliato: né troppo stretta da altre mani, con un aspetto d'innocenza, malgrado il lusso delle sue gemme' (1:33).

13. For a discussion of the hand as semiotic indicator, see Paolo Valesio, 'The Practice of Literary Semiotics: A Theoretical Proposal.'

14. Not all clues are so complicated, e.g., the analysis of finger-

prints. This kind of straightforward clue analysis found its way into fiction in 1894 in Mark Twain's tale, 'Puddin'head Wilson,' after Sir Francis Galton wrote some treatises on the analysis of fingerprints between 1888 and 1892 (Galton, *Fingerprints*). Even fingerprints, however, are a trace left by a body, not an actual part of it.

15. Umberto Eco, *A Theory of Semiotics*, 223–24.

16. 'In Rachele Cabib brillava tutta l'alta beltà muliebre giudaica. Così certo, nei tempi patriarcali, le sue antenate dovevano essere belle, nate al sole della Mesopotamia, erranti per le valli fiorite e arrestantisi alle fresche fontane: così doveva essere Rebecca, la nobile fanciulla: così Erodiade, colei che fatalmente strappò al Tetrarca la testa di Giovanni Batista. Rachele era alta e snella della persona e nelle sue forme erano una grazia e una seduzione infinite: ogni sua movenza aveva un senso armonico che completava la purezza delle sue linee. Era pallida e un po' bruna, ma bruno di avorio, caldo e vivido, carnagione ammirabile, dove il sangue della giovinezza e della salute scorreva, vigoroso e fine, insieme. Nerissimi i capelli e profondamente neri gli occhi, tagliati a mandorla, socchiusi sotto le palpebre d'avorio dalle lunghe ciglia ricurve: e negli occhi una espressione misteriosa di pensiero, un segreto impenetrabile che destava una curiosità sempre inappagata. Il volto era ovale, in una linea molle e carezzevole: la bocca era rossa e tumida, un po' fiera, poco fatta pel sorriso e per le parole. Bellissima!' (1:45–46).

17. 'L'uomo che ha rapito a Dio il segreto di dominare la volontà umana, il più glorioso figliuolo d'Israele, dopo Mosè' (2:247).

18. Sarah's precise age at the birth of Isaac is not agreed on by Biblical scholars: estimates range between ninety and one hundred.

19. In an interesting reversal here that forms a pattern in this text, conversion to Judaism does require a change of name. The convert takes on a Hebrew name and sometimes abandons his or her former name entirely. The naming in this text becomes confused by the end of the long, two-volume work. In Henner's confession, which comes at the very end of the text, we are told that Maria's Jewish name was Miriam. Yet she is called Sara by Mosè in

the first part of the novel. Either the author simply forgot what Jewish name she had used for the character at the beginning of the novel, or the fact that Mosè refers to Maria as Sara and not Miriam has a deliberate symbolic significance.

20. 'Quella sovranità che non possiede più il popolo d'Israele, io avrei potuto restaurarla, col mio potere e coi soccorsi dei grandi milionari ebrei: io avrei potuto mettermi a capo del mio popolo!' (2:250).

21. 'Ma fra le sessantamila persone che dimorano nelle sacre muraglie, vi è, forse, un popolo di Gerusalemme? Chi meriterà, dunque, questo nome eletto, invidiato dagli altri popoli e caro al Signore?

Non gli ebrei che formano, oramai, la metà, oltre la metà, degli abitanti di Gerusalemme. Israele aveva avuto, dono incommensurabile, una divina promessa, aveva avuto la sublime realtà del più grande avvenire che sia serbato a un popolo: ma si stancò di esser pio, buono, felice. Dal fatale giovedì di Nisam, in cui gli ebrei, bizzarramente furenti e ciechi di furore contro il Nazareno, vollero, essi vollero, che il sangue di quel Giusto cadesse sulle lore teste e su quelle dei loro figliuoli, la invocata maledizione li colpì e furon dispersi, e non furono più nè una nazione, nè un popolo ... gli ebrei hanno ricominciato a tornare a Gerusalemme. Vi ritornano da tutti i paesi di Europa, pallidi, stanchi, quasi sempre malaticci, con aria timida di cani frustati, sogguardando obliquamente ogni persona, temendo in oguno un nemico, un persecutore, taciturni, pensosi, incapaci di disputare ... si distinguono, sovra tutto, a un aspetto costante di debolezza, d'infermità, anche nei giovani, anche nei bimbi.' Matilde Serao, *Il paese di Gesù*, 79–80.

22. For a discussion of the image of the Jew as diseased, see Gilman, *Jewish Self-Hatred*, esp. 74–75.

23. Deanna Shemek, in 'Prisoners of Passion: Women and Desire in Matilde Serao's Romanzi D'Amore,' asserts that Marcus Henner 'resembles such real and literary figures of the nineteenth century as Sigmund Freud, George Du Maurier's Svengali, and E. T. A. Hoffman's Sandman' (254).

24. 'Il Maestro era seduto nel vecchio seggiolone di Mosè Cabib e la piccola persona deforme e rattrappita si perdeva in

quell'ampia seggiola. Teneva le mani sui bracciali di pelle nera e nella penombra sembravano bianche e rigide come quella di un mostro. Malgrado la poca luce, si vedeva un volto veramente orribile, più che pallido, scialbo; con gli zigomi sporgenti e le mascelle prominenti; senza un pelo sulle labbra e con radi peli brizzolati e incolti, sulle guance; una bocca tagliata diritta, come una ferita netta netta, con le labbra sottili di un roseo che andava al cresimi; con una tastiera di denti grossi e giallastri; con una fronte sfuggente, su cui si ergeva una capigliatura bizzarra, di capelli quasi rossi, ma fini e incolti, anche essi, quindi intrigati come una boscaglia: e infine quegli occhi verdi, verdi, verdi come l'acqua verde, gelidi, fulminei talvolta e talvolta semplicemente vitrei. Il corpo era deforme: una gobba sulla spalla sinistra contorceva quel torace enorme su quelle gambe corte, sottili, ignobili. Era orribile' (1:123).

25. 'Ma specialmente sui cristiani, io ho esercitato tutta la mia forza dell'ipnotista e tutti i segreti della magìa di mia madre. Ah, come li ho odiati bene questi cristiani e come li ho polverizzati, tutti quelli che sono capitati sotto la mia volontà! Come ho spezzato i loro cuori e rovinato le loro esistenze, senza che essi potessero intendere tutta la mia vendetta!' (2:253).

26. 'Era una vendetta annosa, quella che esercitavo contro loro, giacchè io era, in fondo, un uomo pio e adoravo il Dio di Abramo e di Mosè; era la vendetta del nostro tempio crollato, della nostra fede precipitata, della nostra nazione dispersa, della nostra fortuna distrutta: la vendetta contro i cristiani, contro queste belve dell'aspetto mite che ci perseguitano da secoli, che non ci danno tregua e che sono, adesso, nei nostri mani, perchè siamo i più ricchi, i più furbi, i più forti, i più audaci' (2:253).

27. 'Uno di quei brutti libracci di questi cristiani' (1:43).

28. P. R. L. Brown, *Relics and Social Status in the Age of Gregory of Tours*.

29. Ibid., 14.

30. 'Egli solo, tenacemente, con una fede incrollabile, aveva creduto che quella mano fosse di persona ancora viva' (2:119).

31. 'Se sapeste che creatura arida, perversa, fredda, odiosa io ero! E se vedeste che anima tenera, pia, mistica, devota, purissima

ho io adesso, perché vi amo, perché la vostra cara mano è venuta sotto le mie labbra!' (2:123).

32. Brown, *Relics,* 8.

33. Ibid.

34. Gilman, *Jewish Self-Hatred.*

35. Ibid., 37–38.

36. 'Una israelita non può essere né l'amante, né la moglie di un cristiano' (1:53); 'Una ebrea può essere fedifraga al marito, non lo è mai con un uomo di un'altra religione' (2:259). Once again, this stereotype of the promiscuity of the Jewish woman is taken from the history of antisemitism. For a discussion, see Gilman, *Jewish Self-Hatred,* 49–50.

Chapter 7: Gender and the Stigma of Difference

1. These passages comprise the first four meanings of stigma listed. There are three other meanings listed as well, ranging from the zoological (respiratory openings in insects; part of the follicle involved in discharging ovum; natural spots or marks), the botanical (part of the pistil in flowering plants that receives the pollen) and the geometrical (a certain point in a plane).

2. The term *stigmata* used in a medical sense was adopted, e.g., by Jean-Martin Charcot, the mid-nineteenth-century doctor who used it to refer to the signs of hysteria in his studies of the female hysteric.

WORKS CITED

Beer, Gillian. *Darwin's Plots: Evolutionary Narrative in Darwin, George Eliot and Nineteenth-Century Fiction.* London: Routledge and Kegan Paul, 1983.

Beller, Steven. *Vienna and the Jews, 1867–1938.* Cambridge: Cambridge University Press, 1989.

Bernheimer, Charles. *Figures of Ill-Repute: Representing Prostitution in Nineteenth-Century France.* Cambridge, Mass.: Harvard University Press, 1989.

Brown, Peter Robert Lamont. *Relics and Social Status in the Age of Gregory of Tours.* Reading: University of Reading, 1977.

Burkhardt, Richard W. 'Closing the Door on Lord Morton's Mare: The Rise and Fall of Telegony.' Pages 1–21 in *Studies in History of Biology* 3, ed. William Coleman and Camille Limoge. Baltimore: Johns Hopkins University Press.

Cavaglion, Alberto. *Otto Weininger in Italia.* Roma: Carucci Editore, 1982.

———. 'Svevo and Weininger (Lord Morton's Horse),' trans. Nancy Harrowitz. In *Jews and Gender: Responses to Otto Weininger,* ed. Nancy Harrowitz and Barbara Hyams. Philadelphia: Temple University Press, forthcoming.

Chamberlin, J. Edward, and Sander Gilman, eds. *Degeneration: The Dark Side of Progress.* New York: Columbia University Press, 1985.

Comas, Juan. 'Racial Myths.' Pages 11–53 in *The Race Question in Modern Science.* London: Unesco and Sidgwick & Jackson, 1956.

Croce, Benedetto. 'Note sulla letteratura italiana nella seconda metà del secolo XIX.' *La critica* 5 (1903): 332.

D'Annunzio, Gabriele. *L'innocente.* Milano: Arnoldo Mondadori, 1940, 1986.

Darwin, Charles. *The Variation of Plants and Animals Under Do-mestication.* Vol.1. New York: Appleton, 1896.

Degler, Carl N. *In Search for Human Nature: The Decline and Revival of Darwinism in American Social Thought.* New York: Oxford University Press, 1991.

Delaney, Janice, Mary Jane Lupton, and Emily Toth. *The Curse: A Cultural History of Menstruation.* Rev. ed. Urbana: University of Illinois Press, 1988.

Dworkin, Andrea. *Right-Wing Women.* New York: Putnam, 1983.

Eco, Umberto. 'Horns, Hooves and Insteps.' Pages 198–220 in *The Sign of Three: Dupin, Holmes, Peirce,* ed. Umberto Eco and Thomas Sebeok. Bloomington: Indiana University Press, 1983.

Eco, Umberto, Maria Federzoni, Isabella Pezzini, and Maria Pia Pozzato. *Carolina Inverzinio, Matilde Serao, Liala.* Florence: La Nuova Italia, 1979.

Eco, Umberto, and Thomas Sebeok, ed. *The Sign of Three: Dupin, Holmes, Peirce.* Bloomington: Indiana University Press, 1983.

Ellis, Havelock. *The Criminal.* London: Scott, 1890; New York: Scribner's, 1907.

Elon, Amos. *Herzl.* New York: Holt, Rinehart & Winston, 1975.

Fanning, Ursula. 'Angel vs. Monster: Serao's Use of the Female Double.' *Italianist* 7 (1987): 63–88.

——. 'Sentimental Subversion: Representations of Female Friendships in the Work of Matilde Serao.' *Annali d'Italianistica* 7 (1989): 273–86.

Freud, Sigmund. 'Fetishism.' Pages 152–57 in *The Standard Edition of the Complete Psychological Works of Sigmund Freud.* Vol.21. London: Hogarth, 1953.

Galton, Francis. *Natural Inheritance.* New York: Macmillan, 1889.

——. *Fingerprints,* New York: Macmillan, 1892.

Gates, Henry Louis, Jr., ed. *'Race,' Writing, and Difference.* Chicago: University of Chicago Press, 1986.

Gilman, Sander. *Difference and Pathology: Stereotypes of Sexuality, Race and Madness.* Ithaca, N.Y.: Cornell University Press, 1985.

———. *Jewish Self-Hatred: Antisemitism and the Hidden Language of the Jews.* Baltimore: Johns Hopkins University Press, 1986.

———. ' "I'm Down on Whores": Race and Gender in Victorian London.' Pages 146–70 in *The Anatomy of Racism,* ed. David Theo Goldberg. Minneapolis: University of Minnesota Press, 1990.

Ginzburg, Carlo. 'Morelli, Holmes, and Freud.' Pages 81–118 in *The Sign of Three: Dupin, Holmes, Peirce,* ed. Umberto Eco and Thomas Sebeok. Bloomington: Indiana University Press, 1983.

Glick, Leonard. 'Types Distinct from Our Own: Franz Boas on Jewish Identity and Assimilation.' *American Anthropologist* 84 (1982): 545–65.

Gould, Steven Jay. *The Mismeasure of Man.* New York: Norton, 1981.

———. *Hen's Teeth and Horse's Toes.* New York: Norton, 1983.

———. 'In Praise of Charles Darwin.' *Proteus* (Fall 1989): 1–4.

Gramsci, Antonio. *Letteratura e vita nazionale.* Torino: Einaudi, 1966.

Gunzberg, Lynn. *Strangers at Home: Jews in the Italian Literary Imagination.* Berkeley and Los Angeles: University of California Press, 1992.

Harrowitz, Nancy. 'The Science of Detection: Epistemology and Materiality in Late Nineteenth Century Italian Mysteries.' Ph.D. dissertation, Yale University, 1986.

Harrowitz, Nancy, and Barbara Hyams, ed. *Jews and Gender: Responses to Otto Weininger.* Philadelphia: Temple University Press, 1994.

Hoberman, John. 'The Myth of Jewish Effeminacy.' *Jews and Gender: Responses to Otto Weininger,* ed. Nancy Harrowitz and Barbara Hyams. Philadelphia: Temple University Press, 1994.

Jacobus, Mary, Evelyn Fox Keller, and Sally Shuttleworth, ed. *Body Politics: Women and the Discourses of Science.* New York: Routledge, 1990.

Janik, Allan. *How Not to Interpret a Culture: Essays on the Problem of Method in the Geisteswissenshaften.* Bergen: Universitetet I Bergen, Filosofisk institutt, Stensilerie Nr. 73, 1986.

Janik, Allan. "Viennese Culture and the Jewish Self-Hatred Hypothesis: A Critique." Pages 75–88 in *Jews, Antisemitism and Culture in Vienna*, ed. Ivar Oxaal, Michael Pollak, and Gerhard Botz. London and New York: Routledge and Kegan Paul, 1987.

Jeuland-Meynaud, Maryse. *Immagini, linguaggio e modelli del corpo nell'opera narrativa di Matilde Serao*. Rome: Edizioni dell'Ateneo, 1986.

Johnson, Barbara. *A World of Difference*. Baltimore: Johns Hopkins University Press, 1987.

Kaplan, Aryeh. *Tefillin*. New York: Union of Orthodox Jewish Congregations of America, 1975.

Katz, Jacob. *Out of the Ghetto*. Cambridge, Mass.: Harvard University Press, 1973.

———. *From Prejudice to Destruction: Antisemitism, 1700–1933*. Cambridge, Mass.: Harvard University Press, 1980.

Kroha, Lucienne. *The Woman Writer in Late Nineteenth-Century Italy: Gender and the Formation of Literary Identity*. Lewiston, N.Y.: Mellon, 1992.

Le Rider, Jacques. *Le cas Otto Weininger: racines de l'antiféminisme et de l'antisemitisme*. Paris: Presses Universitaires de France, 1982.

Leatherdale, Clive. *Dracula: The Novel and the Legend*. Wellingborough, Northhamptonshire: Aquarian, 1985.

Levi, Giulio Augusto. 'Ottone Weininger.' *La Voce*, February 10, 1910, p.261.

Loewenstein, Andrea Freud. *Loathsome Jews and Engulfing Women: Metaphors of Projection in the Works of Wyndham Lewis, Charles Williams, and Graham Greene*. New York: NYU Press, 1993.

Lombroso, Cesare. *L'antisemitismo e le scienze moderne*. Torino, Roma: L. Roux e C. Editori, 1894.

———. *Genio e degenerazione: nuovi studi e nuove battaglie*. Milano, Paris: Remo Sandron, 1898 (first ed., Palermo, 1897).

Lombroso, Cesare, and Guglielmo Ferrero. *La donna delinquente, la prostituta e la donna normale*. Torino: Fratelli Bocca Editori, 1903.

Lombroso-Ferrero, Gina. *Criminal Man*. Montclair, N.J.: Patterson Smith, 1972.

Marcus, Paul, and Alan Rosenberg. "Another Look at Jewish Self-Hatred." Pages 37–59 in *Journal of Reform Judaism*, 36, no. 3 (summer 1989).

Mehlman, Jeffrey. Review of Sander Gilman's *Jewish Self-Hatred: Antisemitism and the Hidden Language of the Jews*, in MLN 102, no. 3 (April 1987): 668–72.

Meyer, Michael A. *Jewish Identity in the Modern World*. Seattle: University of Washington Press, 1990.

Müller-Hill, Benno. *Murderous Science*. Oxford: Oxford University Press, 1988.

Oden, Robert. 'Religious Identity and the Sacred Prostitution Accusation.' *Bible without Theology*. San Francisco: Harper and Row, 1987.

Olrik, Hilde, 'Le sang impur: Notes sur le prostituée de Lombroso.' *Romantisme: Revue du dix-neuxième siècle* 31 (1981): 167–78.

Pearson, Karl. *The Life, Letters and Labours of Francis Galton*. Cambridge: Cambridge University Press, 1924.

Porter, Jack Nusan. *The Jew as Outsider*. Washington, D.C.: University Press of America, 1981.

Russett, Cynthia Eagle. *Sexual Science: The Construction of Victorian Womanhood*. Cambridge, Mass.: Harvard University Press, 1989.

Schilardi, Wanda De Nunzio. 'L'antifemminismo di Matilde Serao.' *La parabola della donna* (Bari: Adriatica Editore, 1983): 272–305.

Schilardi, Wanda De Nunzio. *Matilde Serao giornalista*. Lecce: Milella Editore, 1986.

Seltzer, Michael, ed. *Kike!: Antisemitism in America*. New York: World, 1972.

Serao, Matilde. 'La politica femminile.' *Corriera di Roma*, April 6, 1887.

———. 'Ma che fanno le femministe?' *Il Giorno*, June 20, 1925.

———. *Il paese di Gesù*. Milano: Fratelli Treves Editori, 1929.

———. *Addio, amore!* Milano: Casa per Edizioni Popolari, 1933.

———. *Castigo*. Milano: Garzanti, 1977.

———. *La mano tagliata*. 2 vols. Firenze: Edizione Salani, 1979.

———. 'Telegrafi dello stato.' *Romanzo della fanciulla.* Napoli: Liguore Editore, 1985.

Shemek, Deanna. 'Prisoners of Passion: Women and Desire in Matilde Serao's Romanzi D'Amore.' Pages 243–54 in *Italiana,* ed. Albert N. Mancini, Paolo Giordano, and Pier Raimondo Baldini. River Forest, Ill.: Rosary College, 1988.

Shuttleworth, Sally. 'Female Circulation: Medical Discourse and Popular Advertising in the Mid-Victorian Era.' Pages 29–46 in *Body/Politics: Women and the Discourses of Science,* ed. Mary Jacobus, Evelyn Fox Keller, and Sally Shuttleworth. New York: Routledge, 1990.

Sontag, Susan. *Illness as Metaphor.* New York: Random House, 1979.

Spackman, Barbara. *Decadent Genealogies: The Rhetoric of Sickness from Baudelaire to D'Annunzio.* Ithaca, N.Y.: Cornell University Press, 1989.

Stoker, Bram. *Dracula.* New York: New American Library, 1965.

Valesio, Paolo. 'The Practice of Literary Semiotics: A Theoretical Proposal.' *Point of Contact – Punto de Contacto* 5 (April–May 1976): 22–41.

Villa, Renzo. *Il deviante ed i suoi segni.* Milano: F. Angeli, 1985.

Warner, Marina. *Alone of All Her Sex: The Myth and the Cult of the Virgin Mary.* New York: Vintage, 1976.

Weininger, Otto. *Geschlecht und Charakter.* Vienna: Wilhelm Braumuller, 1903.

———. *Sex and Character.* New York and Chicago: Burt, 1906.

Wisse, Ruth R. *If I Am Not for Myself: The Liberal Betrayal of the Jews.* New York: Free Press, 1992.

Wolf, Leonard. *Annotated Dracula.* London: New English Library, 1975.

Yamauchi, Edwin M. 'Cultic Prostitution: A Case Study in Cultural Diffusion.' Pages 213–22 in *Orient and Occident,* ed. Harry A. Hoffner, Jr. Neukirchen-Vluyn: Neukirchen, 1973.

INDEX